CONFRONTING
INEQUALITY

CONFRONTING
INEQUALITY

THE SOUTH AFRICAN CRISIS

EDITED BY MICHAEL NASSEN SMITH

Fanele

(Zul; Xho; Tso): necessary.
This is a necessary book.

First published by Fanele, an imprint of Jacana Media (Pty) Ltd in 2018

10 Orange Street
Sunnyside
Auckland Park 2092
South Africa
+2711 628 3200
www.jacana.co.za

ISBN 978-1-928232-73-5

Cover design by Shawn Paikin and Maggie Davey
Editing and proofreading by Lara Jacob
Index by Josh Bryson
Layout by Alexandra Turner
Set in Stempel Garamond 10/14.5pt
Job no. 003414

Printed by **novus print**, a Novus Holdings company

See a complete list of Jacana titles at www.jacana.co.za

'Our conversations must be underscored by the realisation that there are real, human lives beneath data and academic terminology. The people most affected by the scourge of inequality must be kept in mind, as we seek to "normalise freedom" and create a country that can truly claim freedom, justice and equality as its reality.'
– Kgalema Motlanthe

Contents

PART 3: THE STRUCTURAL DIMENSIONS OF INEQUALITY
IN SOUTH AFRICA

PREFACE

Michael Nassen Smith

Background

A RECENT WORLD BANK REPORT paints a desperate picture of poverty and inequality in South Africa. Poverty levels are unsustainably high and unemployment, which the report identifies as the key challenge for the South African economy, was at a whopping 27.7% in 2017. The labour market is still characterised by large racial and gender disparities (World Bank, 2018: xiv). Seventy-six per cent of South Africans face an imminent threat of falling below the poverty line. Millions do not have access to food, healthcare, decent sanitation and other essentials of a dignified life.

Since the transition, South Africa has not made much progress in addressing the vast social chasms emerging from our history. In fact, the democratic era has witnessed widening inequality. South Africa remains one of the most unequal countries in the world. Depending on the source, the country's Gini coefficient has hovered between 0.63 and 0.68 since 2010. Only two other countries, Botswana and Namibia, have reached the 0.6 mark in the same period (see Makgetla in this volume). In terms of wealth, the top percentile of households held 70.9% of the nation's wealth while the bottom 60% held a mere 7% in the period between 2008 and 2015 (World Bank, 2018: xvi).

South Africa is intolerably unequal in terms of income; yet measuring on the axis of wealth takes things well beyond the pale.

While the poor continue to suffer, the rich have seemingly prospered. Between 2007 and 2017, the cumulative holdings of the top ten earners on the Johannesburg Stock Exchange (JSE) increased from R64bn to R280bn. The average remuneration of the top 200 earners increased from R16.6m in 2007 to R20.8m in 2015. The highest paid members of the richest listed firms earned between 120 and 1,332 times more than average pay (see McGregor and Francis & Massie in this volume).

These are the statistics which help to explain the continued presence of tension and protest in the country and a general sense that the legacies of apartheid and colonialism have not been overcome. A recent report has confirmed that the structure of the economy has largely remained intact since the apartheid era. It has called for a reappraisal of the political compromises struck in 1994 and the formulation of a new path towards reindustrialisation and an inclusive society (Bell et al, 2018). It is with these facts in mind that we have collected a series of papers designed to serve as a catalyst to confront inequality in South Africa. This should be seen as part of a broader effort to realise the promise of democracy.

This volume is situated within the explosion of interest in inequality studies since the publication of Thomas Piketty's *Capital in the 21st Century*. Piketty's debunking of the dominant orthodox consensus on inequality caused quite a stir in intellectual, popular and policymaking circles, but inviting numerous critical commentaries too. And although his analysis is confined to the Global North, it has attracted the attention of academics, policymakers and civil society actors in the Global South, including South Africa. Piketty himself has admitted that the most significant weakness of his work is what he calls its 'Western-centred' frame (Piketty, 2017). In that sense, it is most pertinent and urgent that the conversation be extended to areas in which the phenomenon is often at its extreme.

Piketty's substantive argument about the causes of inequality has attracted a number of critical appraisals, with many social scientists (on both the left and right) questioning a number of its pillars. Yet, even where analysts have disagreed with the form of his argument, there has been a broad acceptance of Piketty's empirical findings and the legitimacy of his warning about the potential social costs of rising inequality (Boushey et al, 2017). Apart from the most conservative environments, inequality, and how to resolve it, is now firmly on the agenda.

There is indeed an emerging global consensus that inequality is a major source of social and political instability. It has been argued that inequality is detrimental for growth and innovation. Being predicated on incumbency and inheritance rather than fair reward for effort, inequality is bad for social cohesion and harmony too. The fact that it is largely reproduced via historical and contemporary forms of prejudice and discrimination – whether in terms of race, gender, nationality and other social markers – is also a cause for alarm. Perhaps one of Piketty's more proactive theses is that inequality poses an existential threat to liberal democracy itself. In a grim vision of a possible future, Piketty imagines a world in which the increasing power of the rich and wealthy will lead to its total domination of the political sphere and the return of the plutocracy that defined the West of the 19th century (Boushey et al, 2017). In short, inequality is an impediment to realising the essence of democracy, social development and human flourishing. Even members of the World Bank and International Monetary Fund (IMF), once apostles of orthodox economics, have acknowledged this fact in various commentaries on the issue (IMF, 2017; World Bank, 2016).

South Africa's history of colonialism and apartheid makes inequality particularly explosive in its context. South Africans are acutely aware of the growing social tensions and violence that typify everyday life and experiences within the country. Our economy is highly concentrated in the hands of a few and shows little sign that it will 'naturally' recover from the deindustrialisation it has experienced since the transition (Bell et al, 2018). For the promise of democracy to be fulfilled, the problem of inequality as experienced by the people need to be confronted and, more broadly, that concerted action be taken to realise the structural transformation of the South African economy and society. We hope that this volume fulfils an intellectual imperative and contributes towards the development of a policy and social agenda for change.

In this volume

The following pages include critical, polemical and academic essays written by researchers, former political leaders and academics. Taken together these essays unpack the origins and causal mechanisms that underpin South African inequality and how that inequality typifies and arranges social life in the country. All papers are 'action oriented' and the reader will be presented with a number of concrete proposals on how to bridge the vast divides that characterise South Africa's economy.[1]

This volume is divided into three broad sections: Part 1 titled 'Political and Social Context: Why Confront Inequality?'; Part 2 titled, 'The Rich and the Poor'; and Part 3 titled 'The Structural Dimensions of Inequality in South Africa'. We close with some brief concluding remarks.

---

1   Versions of several of these papers were originally presented at the IFAA Confronting Inequality Conference in 2017. The conference also included presentations by Marissa Gerards (former Netherlands ambassador to South Africa and Dr Gwen Ramokgoba (Deputy Health Minister of South Africa) whose papers are not published in this volume. You can find copies of all the presentations delivered at the conference online: https://ifaaza.org/2017/10/17/presentations-from-confronting-inequality-conference/

Part 1 includes contributions from the director of the Institute for African Alternatives (IFAA), Ben Turok, former president Kgalema Motlanthe and former public protector Thuli Madonsela.

Turok demands that South Africans be more forthright and unambiguous about the depths of our inequality issue and embark on an ambitious research and social agenda to resolve it. He argues that inequality is embedded in South Africa's social structure as a symptom of the history of apartheid and colonialism. Nonetheless, it is reproduced by policy error and indecisiveness in contemporary times. In Europe, he says, inequality was beaten by a militant working-class movement, which applied pressure in the corridors of power. He wonders why this is not happening in the context of post-apartheid democratic South Africa.

Motlanthe's essay suggests that South Africans do not have an adequate understanding of inequality and calls for more research into its causes, characteristics and social impact. Since current policy frameworks to address inequality have clearly failed, in his view what is needed is a renewed effort to address social and economic inequities, with a revitalisation of basic education at the centre. In addition, Motlanthe warns that inequality cannot be resolved without addressing 'state capture' in all of its manifestations, which will require all facets of South African society to engage in the vigorous protection of our democratic institutions.

Thuli Madonsela's contribution is situated in reflections on the legacy of the anti-apartheid struggle. She laments the slow progress made in realising the vision of The Freedom Charter, a document she suggests still carries the aspirations of the masses of South Africa's poor and disenfranchised. Madonsela argues that the continued existence of racialised inequality gives ammunition to nefarious and anti-democratic forces, represented most recently by the Bell Pottinger-sponsored 'white monopoly capital' campaign. While noting the fragility of race relations and the legitimate fear that redistributive efforts could be used to legitimate narrow elite accumulation and corruption, Madonsela nonetheless urges that South Africa undertake ambitious structural reforms of its society and economy.

Part 2 has contributions from Andrew McGregor, David Francis and Kaylan Massie.

McGregor, managing director of *WhoOwnsWhom*, begins the section by providing a snapshot of earnings inequality sourced from data on the Johannesburg Stock Exchange (JSE). McGregor's brief yet provocative account of the earnings of the extremely rich as compared with the rest of the population is vivid illustration of South Africa's economic inequities.

McGregor's work provides a useful framing for David Francis and Kaylan Massie's comprehensive study of wage inequality in South Africa. Francis and Massie argue that inequality is perhaps the most damaging socio-economic problem confronting South Africa. Wage inequality is the single largest driver of inequality and this has deepened over the democratic era. Francis and Massie identify what they call a 'broken and distorted labour market', which systematically benefits the small elite at the expense of the lowly paid. This labour market also continues to reproduce patterns of racial and gender inequities. The authors explore a number of policy options that might address these issues including pay caps, pay disclosures and other equalising devices.

Part 3 includes contributions from Neva Makgetla, Pali Lehohla, Ivan Turok, and Murray Leibbrant, Simone Schotte and Rocco Zizzamia.

Makgetla traces the historical foundations of inequality in South Africa and demonstrates how apartheid-era, state-sanctioned discrimination continues to shape the country's economic landscape. She considers the efforts that the post-apartheid state has taken to reducing inequality and finds disappointing results even as ambitious redistributive programmes have been initiated. The democratic system, she argues, has maintained the fundamental inequities of the old regime, even as the higher income group has become more representative in terms of race and gender. This inequality persists due to deeply concentrated economic power that is reinforced by inequities in education, residence infrastructure and work organisation.

Next is a summary of a StatsSA report written by former statistician general Pali Lehohla that underscores the failure to address South Africa's historical inequities in the post-apartheid era. Lehohla bemoans the failure of the democratic government to take advantage of a demographic dividend. The potential for a demographic dividend arises when a country experiences a long-term increase in its working-age ratio, which is the percentage of its population that is of working age (15–64 years). This increase should, in theory, translate into economic prosperity. Yet, Lehohla demonstrates how the post-apartheid state failed to create supporting conditions needed to maximise the potential benefits of a demographic transition experienced since the collapse of apartheid. Inequality has been exacerbated by this failure. This summary is written by Zunaid Moola, the deputy editor of *New Agenda: South African Journal of Social and Economic Policy*.

Ivan Turok argues that there has been a tendency to neglect the spatial dimensions (or geography) of poverty and inequality. The existence of extreme spatial disparities is partly a legacy of racial separation imposed under colonialism and apartheid – which saw land dispossession on a massive scale combined with forced removals, residential controls, segregation and vastly unequal education systems – and partly a result of inadequate spatial policy frameworks in the post-apartheid era. These geographic inequities are reinforced by contemporary patterns of economic concentration, physical infrastructure imbalances and a lack of equitably dispersed institutional capabilities. For Turok, South Africans are growing up in 'different worlds', with profoundly unequal access to social and physical infrastructure and opportunities.

Finally, we conclude this section with an essay from Leibbrandt, Schotte and Zizzamia, which analyses how poverty, inequality and unemployment sustain themselves in a symbiotic fashion. Economic opportunities, they argue, have much to do with socio-economic status of the family South Africans find themselves born into. In other words, advantage and disadvantage is largely inherited. The authors identify a volatile phenomenon of 'precarious mobility'. A significant amount of the population has high probabilities of moving across the poverty line. It is important to underscore the word 'temporary' here. Many South Africans are highly vulnerable to falling into the poverty line over time. The authors propose a social stratification schema consisting of five classes that would capture the mobility patterns and vulnerabilities in the population. They argue that state support, especially to the chronic poor who stand little chance of falling into the formal economy and escaping poverty, is crucial to addressing poverty, inequality and unemployment.

The concluding remarks attempts to a suggest a way forward to confront inequality in South Africa based on the work presented in this volume and other reflections. We hope this volume enriches the conversation about inequality in South Africa while also encouraging various social forces, particularly those embedded in the struggles of the poor and marginalised, to take up the challenge of realising a prosperous and just future.

I would like to thank the Royal Netherlands Embassy for their generous funding contribution towards the publication of this volume of essays. Thanks are also extended to Ben Turok, Carilee Osborne, Rekang Jankie, and Shamielah Booley who assisted with the production of this volume.

References

Bell, J., Goga, S., Mondliwa, P. & Roberts, S. 2018. 'Structural transformation in South Africa: Moving towards a smart, open economy for all.' Industrial Development Think Tank (IDTT). Available at: https://static1. squarespace.com/static/52246331e4b0a46e5f1b8ce5/t/5ad9 e4baf950b767531fe8a9/1524229357942/IDTT+Structural+ Transformation+in+South+Africa+Moving+towards+a+ smart%2C+open+economy+for+all.pdf [Accessed on 1 August 2018].

Boushey, H., B. de Long & M. Steinhum (eds.) *After Piketty: The Agenda for Economics and Inequality*. Cambridge: Harvard University Press.

International Monetary Fund. 2017. *Fiscal Monitor: Tackling Inequality.* Washington: International Monetary Fund. Available at: http://www.imf. org/en/publications/fm/issues/2017/10/05/fiscal-monitor-october-2017 [Accessed on 15 October 2018].

Piketty, T. 2017. 'Towards a reconciliation between economics and the social sciences', in H. Boushey, B. de Long & M. Steinhum (eds.) *After Piketty: The Agenda for Economics and Inequality*. Cambridge: Harvard University Press.

World Bank. 2018. *Overcoming Poverty and Inequality in South Africa.* Washington: World Bank. Available at: http://documents.worldbank.org/ curated/en/530481521735906534/pdf/124521-REV-OUO-South-Africa-Poverty-and-Inequality-Assessment-Report-2018-FINAL-WEB.pdf [Accessed on 15 October 2018].

World Bank. 2016. *Poverty and Shared Prosperity: Taking on Inequality.* Washington: World Bank. Available at: https://openknowledge.worldbank. org/bitstream/handle/10986/25078/9781464809583.pdf [Accessed on 15 October 2018].

PART 1

THE POLITICAL AND SOCIAL CONTEXT: WHY CONFRONT INEQUALITY?

SOUTH AFRICANS SHOULD NOT BE POLITE ABOUT INEQUALITY

Ben Turok

THERE IS NOW A BROAD AGREEMENT that South Africa's critical social problems lie in three areas – unemployment, poverty and inequality. There is hardly a single report that does not give these issues priority. The unemployment problem is straightforward: Jobs have to be created and the solutions are well understood. Poverty is well documented and we all know that poverty is a function of unemployment and that it can be alleviated by social grants. But there is a limit beyond which this all becomes unsustainable.

Dealing with inequality is a different matter because it is deeply embedded in the social structure of our society. This is obviously a legacy of the rigors and discriminations of apartheid, at least in part. Inequality cannot be addressed by welfare measures or even by taxation alone. Inequality stares us in the face every way we turn in our daily lives. It is prominent where we work, where we live, indeed in every daily experience. It is so great a part of our national experience that it is almost impossible to conceive of any measures we could take to remove its most obvious tentacles. It is all pervasive and undermines our efforts at nation building. In some respects, gross class inequality is as undermining as racial discrimination, though of course the two are linked.

Even the World Bank, not renowned for giving salience to normative issues, has recently given much prominence to inequality. In its report, *Overcoming Poverty and Inequality in South Africa*, the Word Bank notes: 'South Africa is not only the most unequal country in the world but inequality has increased since the end of apartheid in 1994' (World Bank, 2018: xv). Moreover, '...between 1993 and 2015, inequality rose in South Africa but fell in each region and the world' (World Bank, 2018: xv).

Even more concerning is that these international comparisons are based on consumption or income date where the Gini coefficient is 0.63. But if inequality in wealth is considered, the Gini is 0.93 which means that inequality in South Africa is way beyond anything else seen in the world. It is the wealth inequality that stares us in the face every day. Here are the statistics:

> *The top percentile of households had 70.9 percent of the wealth and the bottom 60 percent had 7.0 percent – richer households are almost ten times wealthier than poor households. What is striking is that ownership of financial assets features prominently among the factors that influence wealth inequality* (World Bank, 2018: xvi).

The report also found that the labour market is split into two extreme types: a small number of highly paid people in the formal sector (mainly large companies) and a much larger number who work in low-paid jobs and that are often informal.

It is such considerations that enable us to say that inequality is structural. It is therefore not open to remedies that are merely palliative, like social grants. Indeed, how can it be when 'for about 76 per cent of the population poverty is a constant threat in their daily lives' (World Bank, 2018: xviii). All this leads the report to an unusual finding: 'Interventions that simultaneously stimulate growth and reduce inequalities are likely to have much more impact than interventions that only stimulate growth or only reduce inequalities' (World Bank, 2018: xxvi).

This is an important departure from the conventional economics of the Bretton Woods institutions, which normally simply promote growth as the solution to all problems. Our government needs to take note. Much as we need foreign investment, much as we need our own private sector to invest the billions stored in the financial agencies and the Johannesburg Stock Exchange (JSE), this is not enough. We need conscious, deliberate measures to tackle inequality wherever it rears its ugly head. And that means everywhere.

We need to address the matter of the wealth tax. The Davis Committee seems to be in favour of such a tax but is delaying possible implementation for understandable reasons. It is clear that the object is not necessarily to raise additional revenue. There is a far more important reason – identified by Piketty himself – and that is that we need to know the scale, location and forms of private wealth.

For inexplicable reasons, the ANC cabinet has never analysed wealth in South Africa, hence there is little data available in the South African Revenue Services (SARS) or the Treasury about wealth. We seem to be embarrassed to talk about the rich and what they do with their money. The best we can do is to suggest that the rich pay enough taxes and that they are too few to make a difference anyway. What is not explained is why there are such huge financial assets in unit trusts, life offices, retirement funds and the JSE. And what about the huge funds that are steadily leaving the country? We find it strange that our universities have paid so little attention to these matters. They seem to prefer the safer terrain of poverty studies, labour markets and the rest, important as they undoubtedly are.

A recent study by Nimrod Zalk suggests that the South African economy is fundamentally a high profit, low-investment economy

(Zalk, 2017). If that is indeed the case, it would explain the extraordinary divisions in our social makeup with a self-contained rich structure standing over a large poor structure. Furthermore, there is evidence of low levels of movement between the two, despite the emergence of some rich black personnel. The rise of the latter social group explains the fact that inequality among black Africans is now greater than in the population as a whole.

Finally, what is puzzling is why the achievement of democracy, which gave voice to the masses and protected the right to strike, has not led to the visible removal of the most obvious inequalities in our society. In Europe, pressures from within the working class brought major social adjustments in capitalist countries. Why not in South Africa?

References

World Bank. 2018. *Overcoming Poverty and Inequality in South Africa.* Washington: World Bank. Available at: http://documents.worldbank. org/curated/en/530481521735906534/pdf/124521-REV-OUO-South-Africa-Poverty-and-Inequality-Assessment-Report-2018-FINAL-WEB.pdf [Accessed on 15 October 2018].

Zalk, N. 2017. 'The things we lost in the fire: The political economy of post-apartheid restructuring of the South African steel and engineering sectors'. PhD thesis, School of Oriental and African Studies, University of London.

THE INEQUALITY DANGER:
THE IMPERATIVE TO NORMALISE FREEDOM

Kgalema Motlanthe

'Countries around the world provide frightening examples of what happens to societies when they reach the level of inequality toward which we are moving. It is not a pretty picture: countries where the rich live in gated communities, waited upon by hordes of low-income workers; unstable political systems where populists promise the masses a better life, only to disappoint. Perhaps most importantly, there is an absence of hope. In these countries, the poor know that their prospects of emerging from poverty, let alone making it to the top, are minuscule. This is not something we should be striving for.' – Joseph Stiglitz, The Price of Inequality

IT IS NOT DIFFICULT TO RELATE the South African present to the picture of a vastly unequal society provided in the opening quote above. Frequent descriptions of contemporary life in South Africa are rooted in a 'tale of two cities' narrative that reveals the stark differences that underscore life within our borders. This is a bleak depiction. But rather than being weighed down by the morass it represents, I am emboldened by the hope that the future that we imagined at the founding of our democracy can be attained.

This hope, however, is not one underscored by naiveté or attempts to disregard the material reality and political circumstances that contribute to its current state. It is born of a shared belief that a better future is possible. Ben Turok's paper for a conference on confronting inequality held by the IFAA in 2017 commences with an unambiguous exploration of the consequences of inequality (Turok, 2017a). It is founded in the belief that when societies, for a vast array of reasons, begin to take the shape of the contours defined by Stiglitz earlier, the threat of violence invades everyday realities and threatens to engulf the better part of the affected world in its long shadow.

Professor Turok emphasises this fact, drawing on the work of French economist Thomas Piketty. At the 2015 Nelson Mandela Annual Lecture, Piketty said:

We also know from historical experience that extreme inequality of the kind of levels we observe in South Africa is not good for development and growth, and it can also lead to violent reactions and violent events. And we all have in mind the very violent episodes at Marikana three years ago, and we know from historical experience that if inequality is not addressed through peaceful means and peaceful democratic institutions it's always potentially a source of violence. And, of course, this can happen again (Piketty, 2015).

The echoes of these statements are found in a recent Oxfam Briefing Paper titled 'An Economy for the 99%', where it notes that:

Left unchecked, growing inequality threatens to pull our

societies apart. It increases crime and insecurity, and undermines the fight to end poverty. It leaves more people living in fear and fewer in hope (Hardoon, 2017).

Frequently, violence is evident in what have been termed 'service delivery protests', but takes wider form. It is evident in continuing commuter bus and taxi unrest. It rears its head in the responses to student protests at our universities. There are numerous ways in which it invades everyday life, and reveals societal rifts that blur the distinctions between the past and the present, perhaps because the past is so present.

A dual economy, in which a formal and informal economy exist side-by-side and creates vastly distinct experiences of citizenship, marks our reality. As a result, we find that the task of fully realising freedom is still one that we have to ardently pursue. Economic marginalisation indeed remains a pressing challenge. With the benefit of hindsight, we can now say that in the initial democratic days, we should have asked this pertinent question: *How do we define the new national cause beyond 1994 and which array of social forces should be mobilised to pursue it?*

There is a simple saying that states 'when you know better, you do better'. While it can be up for critique, perhaps we can rephrase this as 'when you know better, you have the capacity to do better.' In briefly considering present research and the gaps that require address, Professor Turok identifies that little research exists on wealth inequality – as analyses of poverty has overwhelmingly been the post-democratic focus (Turok, 2017a). Orthofer (2016) agrees that existing research on inequality has focused almost exclusively on income. These assertions are supported by Piketty who stressed that our aim should be to 'contribute to a more informed democratic discussion about inequality' (Piketty, 2015). We need to consider income *and* wealth in relation to poverty, and reflect on how this affects employment opportunities, movement and residence, access to adequate healthcare and education and the way that everyday business is conducted. It is clear that a larger picture needs to be attained that gives a greater in-depth view on the factors affecting present inequality.

Dealing with the failure of formal rights to realise substantive rights requires that we prioritise the maintenance of the mechanisms and institutions that help us to fully realise democracy. As we strive to address inequality and its racially skewed dimensions, it would be remiss not to consider the roles and responsibilities of the institutions of democracy.

The current state of our institutions is shaped by historical forces. It has become evident that we are faced with a widespread crisis of democratic institutions. These sites include government, public universities and the private sector. The term 'state capture' continues to dominate public discourse around governance, which delineates how the interference of nepotistic relations and tainted business transactions can affect the workings of the state and inability of government to meet its social responsibilities. Any interventions that seek to address inequality cannot ignore this reality. We are required to both question and critique the government's role in alleviating poverty, inequality and unemployment, as well as considering our collective responsibility and agency in contributing towards rebuilding our society on new terms.

We also know, from the work of many economists and social theorists, that multiple factors influence the present state of inequality. These include the state of the global economy, the present design of the economic system, historical and structural features of our political economy, and unearned benefits that accompany various forms of privilege. What then could be the possible way out of this bleak picture?

Professor Turok (2017b) writes:

Current mechanisms of welfare grants and public spending are not doing enough to confront inequality in our economy. Other more ambitious solutions may be needed to resolve the structural constraints that continue to frustrate inclusive development.

Our current policy framework clearly fails to fully comprehend and address present challenges in inequality. Yet, in keeping a solutions-oriented mindset, I offer one site that must be considered: Education. The introduction of the Bantu Education Act of 1953 stratified the quality of South African education along a racial hierarchy. It was designed to ensure that certain parts of the citizenry would not be productive in the economy. The present effect of this is evident in the Statistician General report on the social profile of vulnerable groups between 2002 and 2012 (Lehohla, 2013). It revealed a startling decline in educational attendance beyond 15 and 16 years of age. This reality significantly affects the country's black and coloured communities. It is important to remember that we are speaking at the level of basic education – which is further complicated by access to higher education and training institutions.

In thinking about inequality, basic education demands our direct address and attention. Failure to access and sustain adequate education skews access to opportunities long after initial enrolment. It touches every aspect of life and has an effect beyond generations. A Stats SA report titled 'Education Series III: Educational enrolment and achievement, 2016' states:

Differences in intergenerational mobility have remained significant across population groups. The same families tend to constitute the most educated group from one generation to the next. Economists refer to this as the under-education trap, as

11

some families remain unskilled from one generation to the next
(Lehohla, 2013).

In conclusion, we cannot map out solutions emboldened only by a set of untested assumptions. This makes this edited volume all the more important as it seeks to understand and present the current data on inequality, the various interpretations on what this data means and a set of solutions that would aid us in realising more democratic alternatives to the status quo. Our conversations must be underscored by the realisation that there are real, human lives beneath data and academic terminology. The people most affected by the scourge of inequality must be kept in mind, as we seek to 'normalise freedom' and create a country that can truly claim freedom, justice and equality as its reality.

References

Hardoon, D. 2017. 'An economy for the 99%', Oxfam Briefing Paper. Available at: https://www.oxfam.org/sites/www.oxfam.org/files/file_attachments/bp-economy-for-99-percent-160117-en.pdf [Accessed on 24 August 2018].

Lehohla, P. 2017. 'Education Series Volume III: Education enrolment and achievement, 2016', Statistics South Africa. Available at: http://www.statssa.gov.za/publications/Report%2092-01-03/Report%2092-01-032016.pdf [Accessed on 24 August 2018].

Lehohla, P. 2013. 'Social profile of vulnerable groups 2002–2012', Statistics South Africa. Available: https://www.statssa.gov.za/publications/Report-03-19-00/Report-03-19-002012.pdf [Accessed on 24 August 2018].

Orthofer, A. 2016. 'Wealth inequality in South Africa: evidence from survey and tax data', REDI 3*3 Working Paper 15. Cape Town: SALDRU.

Piketty, T. 2015. 'Transcript of Nelson Mandela Annual Lecture 2015.' Nelson Mandela Foundation. Available at: https://www.nelsonmandela.org/news/entry/transcript-of-nelson-mandela-annual-lecture-2015

[Accessed on 24 August 2018].

Turok, B. 2017a. 'We have work to do on inequality', Daily Maverick. Available at: https://www.dailymaverick.co.za/opinionista/2017-07-26-we-have-work-to-do-on-inequality/ [Accessed on 12 August 2018].

Turok, B. 2017b. 'Confronting inequality in South Africa', Institute for African Alternatives. Available at: https://ifaaza.org/2017/07/11/confronting-inequality/ [Accessed on 20 August 2018].

CONFRONTING INEQUALITY: THOUGHTS ON PUBLIC ACCOUNTABILITY AND POLICY RESONANCE

Thuli Madonsela

IFAA's CONFRONTING INEQUALITY conference of 2017 was timely, as inequality and poverty in our country and the world are at their highest. Extreme poverty and inequality are not only unjust but also a major threat to peace and stability. The response of the United Nations (UN) is to rally countries around Sustainable Development Goals. Providing the platform for deliberating on inequality in all its forms must be applauded.

A polarising campaign
In South Africa the task to confront inequality was recently hijacked by a company based in the United Kingdom, which engineered a vicious and racially divisive campaign that caught the imagination of many South Africans. Black people, who remain structurally unequal to their white counterparts, regarding income, wealth and access to private social services and social capital, were particularly vulnerable to this campaign. Using catch phrases such as 'white monopoly capital' (WMC) and 'radical economic transformation',

the initiative ran mostly on social media platforms and Gupta/Zuma-owned mainstream media platforms such as the ANN7 TV channel and *The New Age* newspaper. Some politicians caught on to the phrases and regularly incorporated them into their speeches. The impact made increasingly fragile race relations more tense.

The campaign, that seemingly confronted the systemic economic exclusion of black people, surfaced just after allegations of state capture emerged and a public protector investigation of the same commenced. The reason for the investigation was the allegation that the Gupta family, which arrived in South Africa from India on the eve of democracy, was engaged in systematic capture and repurposing of the presidency, state owned enterprises (SOEs) and other organs of state, particularly those responsible for law enforcement and state security. The family's purpose was their own rapid economic advancement at the expense of the South African state and the evasion of accountability. They would achieve this through leveraging their social and economic relationship with the president and his son, with whom they co-owned key companies.

I am certain that many are now breathing a sigh of relief that Bell Pottinger has been held accountable by the UK PR peer agency. Many now believe that we can now 'go back to normal' whatever that may be.

Collateral value

But can we go back to normal? What is normal?

Are we not at a risk of similar attacks on our democracy through the exploitation of raw feelings around socio-economic exclusion? Particularly as these feelings are a result of race- and gender-based accumulated socio-economic advantage? In other words, isn't inequality a problem we should all be concerned about? The UN and the African Union, among others, all agree that we should all be concerned about inequality.

There is a growing body of data showing that extreme inequality and poverty is not only a threat to peace and stability but also impedes development. That makes sense to me. Structural inequality translates into structural inefficiency in the utilisation of human capital. Regarding gender inequality, the International Monetary Fund (IMF) and the World Bank, among others, have conducted studies that prove conclusively that leaving women behind socially and economically weighs down a country and undermines its GDP (Kochhar, Jani-Chandra & Newiak, 2017; Hakura et al, 2016; Wood & De La Briere, 2018). I hope you agree with me that we don't need rocket science to extend the same logic to other forms of socio-economic exclusion including race, disability and age. It seems to me that we could draw collateral value and lessons from the toxic campaign that attempted to take advantage of our economic inequality for nefarious purposes. A possible lesson is that racial reconciliation remains fragile at the level of relationships and integration. We must also admit that structural and systemic inequality remains a reality.

The overwhelming response to Bell Pottinger's incitement (which in reality was the proverbial 'dead cat' aimed at deflecting attention from the serious 'state capture' allegations) tells us that poverty makes it easier to ignite extremism. Who will forget the young people acting as a vigilante group, hounding the public protector's office and hysterically demanding that the state capture investigation be dropped or at least broadened to a meaningless search for anything and everything against white businesses that have engaged with or lobbied state functionaries?

Socio-economic inequality

Statistics South Africa (Stats SA) recently announced that extreme poverty and inequality are growing in the country. Of greater concern is that the number of persons said to be living in extreme poverty (that section of our population who live on less than R441 per person per month), rose from 11 million people in 2011 to 13.8 million in 2015. This is a step back to the level of extreme poverty that was present in 2007 (Lehohla, 2017).

Statistics further show that more than 30.4 million, that is, more than half of the country's 55 million people, live in poverty, which increased from 53.2% to 55.5% between 2006 and 2015. Unemployment is at its peak at about 28% officially and about 36%, unofficially. The statistics show that the most vulnerable are children below the age of 17 (Lehohla, 2017).

But poverty statistics don't do justice to the ugly reality of poverty. They don't provide visuals or put a human face to the problems. A visit to Tidimala lower primary school about 45 kilometres from Pretoria brought us face to face with the impact of poverty, its indignity and how it contributes to long-term underdevelopment of children from poor households. At Tidimala and Sizabantwana primary schools, which we visited under the auspices of the Tutu Desk Foundation, we were confronted with the harsh reality of how the other half lives. This extreme poverty is juxtaposed with the fact that some of our country's business luminaries, including from historically disadvantaged groups, proudly feature in the global *Forbes* magazine list of dollar billionaires. I am deeply concerned that this takes place in a context in which there is not enough interest on the issues of poverty and inequality in our country.

Deferred democracy dream

In chapter 4 of her book, *No Longer Whispering to Power*, Thandeka Gqubule, with whom I was detained without trial during apartheid, nostalgically refers to the dream of 'another country' that propelled us to step out and push back against apartheid. While the story is about the beauty of the dreams that drive the struggle, the narrative is also an indictment of the sad reality of similar excesses of the powerful that we thought would be buried with apartheid.

The outcome of the struggle was supposed to be a democracy that works for all with no one left behind. Part of the deal was also that no one would be above the law and no one would be deprived of equal protection under the law. 'The people shall govern,' boldly declared The Freedom Charter, a document developed by diverse progressives from the African National Congress and its allies in 1955 to outline the vision of the new country beyond apartheid. The gathering on its own was an act of courage as was the boldness of the vision behind its provisions. It embraced the notion of democracy being about the government of the people, by the people, for the people.

It is worth noting that in a true democracy, the power must lie with the people. *Demos* is a Greek word that means people and *cratos*, in the same language means power. Democracy, accordingly, should translate to people's power exercised collectively and directly or through people's representatives equally chosen by the people. Equally important and often forgotten is that, 'for the people' means that the fruits of democracy must be enjoyed by all. Ultimately, democracy should expand the frontiers of human freedom. It should give everyone optimum conditions to be the best they could be and in return, to serve the collective and humanity at large, the best way they can.

Bridging the gap between the dream and reality

Kwame Nkrumah spelt out the ideal manner in which the fruits of freedom from colonialism and democracy should be enjoyed by all. In a 1957 broadcast he said:

> *We shall measure our progress by the improvement in the health of our people; by the number of children in school, and by the quality of their education; by the availability of water and electricity in our towns and villages, and* by the happiness which our people take in being able to manage their own affairs. *The welfare of our people is our chief pride, and it is by this that my Government will ask to be judged* (emphasis mine) (Nkrumah, 1957).

A few years later, in another address, Nkrumah added:

> *We have the blessing of the wealth of our vast resources, the power of our talents and the potentialities of our people. Let us grasp now the opportunities before us and meet the challenge to our survival* (Nkrumah, 1965).

This promise is similar to the one in the preamble to the South African Constitution, which seeks to build a united nation where everyone's potential is freed and life improved. Yet, there is clearly a gap between reality and the constitutional promise. Elsewhere I have admitted that the past continues to influence the present. The accumulated socio-economic advantages for white people and accumulated socio-economic disadvantages for black people, women and other disadvantaged people undoubtedly remain with us. But can we legitimately only blame apartheid as many politicians do and particularly did at the height of the 'white monopoly capital' campaign?

19

Getting a societal buy-in regarding compensatory measures

The Truth and Reconciliation Commission (TRC) did great work in healing key wounds inflicted by apartheid brutality. But in my considered view that reconciliation project was abandoned too soon.

Part of racial polarisation today is reflected in white anger and despair over affirmative action and Black Economic Empowerment (BEE). Apart from the fact that both often hide nepotism, cronyism and plain corruption, many, particularly from historically advantaged communities, do not appreciate the rationale behind some of the remedial measures that seek to redress systemic historical disparities, on the grounds of race, gender and disability.

A friend of mine demonstrates accumulated socio-economic inequality to young people by using a race between two groups. One group wearing one colour is forbidden from starting while another group wearing a different colour is allowed to run as far and fast as they can, assisted and supported by the managers. At some point both groups are told to stop where they are and it is announced that they are now equal and everyone can now run as fast as they can to the finish line, regardless of where they started from. Í have used this example effectively to help economically privileged groups to understand the cry behind the #FeesMustFall protest and the anger it generated among students.

Maladministration, including the wastage regularly identified by the auditor general and the public protector, is also a factor behind failure to significantly reduce poverty and inequality. Without maladministration and corruption, there would be money for basic minimum education infrastructure in all schools and other constitutional promises. For every public rand dishonestly and unlawfully siphoned into private pockets, as alleged for example in state capture, there is less available for the inclusive development agenda that improves the quality of life for all and unleashes the potential inherent in all our citizens.

We should be particularly concerned about the apparent weakening of the rule of law. While our courts, as led by the Constitutional Court, have done a sterling job in upholding their role as ultimate guardians of the Constitution, the same cannot be said about the appetite of law enforcement agencies, such as the Hawks, Asset Forfeiture Unit (AFU) and the National Prosecuting Authority, to bring alleged corruption culprits to book. A particularly shocking example is the time it is taking to limit potential 'state capture' damage, including possible permanent loss of stolen state funds and erosion of evidence trails. This delay is occurring despite a report of the public protector released over a year ago and numerous media exposés, particularly under what has been termed the 'Gupta Leaks'.

What are we to do?

The long-term view requires a review of current and past policies to assess the extent to which they have the capacity to reduce poverty and inequality. Reducing inequality and poverty will require helping the marginalised to earn incomes and reducing wealth and income inequality between groups. For income to be generated, there must be growth. But I do not believe either must come first. They should happen concurrently. A reinforcing process will be the pursuit of equality between nations, including arresting illicit capital outflows and reviewing trade deals that disadvantage South Africa. In this regard, careful examination of BRICS import–export deals is important to ensure the country does not become a footstool of its stronger partners.

I am sure we can all agree that this cannot be government's sole responsibility. Is it not high time that we all joined hands to craft and execute something akin to the post-Second World War M-Plan, to advance socio-economic inclusion in a systematic way? Such a plan would supplement, and elaborate on, the National Development Plan (NDP).

Women who gathered this year under the themes, 'Women leading the healing of the division of the past' and 'Women leading socio-economic inclusion' on 9 and 26 August 2017 respectively said yes to this idea. The two meetings produced a draft road map to realise this. The process sought to leverage social capital in civil society, including business, to voluntarily reduce inequalities and poverty. It pointed out that we need to arrest corruption urgently. The starting point in this regard should be to claw back the money from state capture allegations where there is clear evidence that public funds have been dishonestly siphoned for personal enrichment or gain. Civil society, particularly academia, also needs to help boost the capacity of the state to design and implement impactable policies regarding inequality and poverty. This includes systematic implementation of sustainable development goals.

It is my sincere view that the call to confront inequality is one of the most critical calls at this stage in our hard-earned constitutional democracy. I further believe that confronting and reducing inequality is everyone's business while good governance, including ending corruption and strengthening accountability and the rule of law, is a must. I am convinced that if we don't act urgently, the next challenge we face will be worse than the toxic 'dead cat' which sought to deflect attention from state capture.

References

Hakura, D., M. Hussain, M. Newiak, V. Thakoor & Fan Yang. 2016. 'Inequality, gender gaps and economic growth: Comparative evidence for sub-saharan Africa', IMF Working Paper WP/16/111. Available at: http://www.imf.org/external/pubs/ft/wp/2016/wp16111.pdf [Accessed on 24 August 2018].

Kochhar, K., S. Jani-Chandra & M. Newiak (eds). 2017. *Women, Work, andEconomic Growth: Levelling the Playing Field.* Washington: International Monetary Fund.

Lehohla, P. 2017. 'Poverty trends in South Africa', *Statistics South Africa.* Available at: https://www.statssa.gov.za/publications/Report-03-10-06 Report-03-10-062015.pdf [Accessed on 15 October 2018].

Nkrumah, K. 1957. Broadcast to the Nation, 24 December 1957.

Nkrumah, K. 1965. Address to the National Assembly, 26 March 1965.

Wood, Q. & B. de la Briere, 2018. 'Unrealized potential: The high cost of gender inequality in earnings', *World Bank: The Cost of Gender Inequality Series.* Available at: https://openknowledge.worldbank.org/ handle/10986/29865 [Accessed on 24 August 2018].

PART 2

THE RICH AND THE POOR

WHO ARE THE RICH:
STOCKS AND TRENDS

Andrew Mcgregor

IN THIS CHAPTER, WE PRESENT THE RESULTS of the research conducted for the *Sunday Times Rich List*. The *Sunday Times Rich List* is an annual publication that ranks South Africa's wealthiest directors and reveals the total value of their investments. It is important to clarify the limitations of this list and the research that went into drawing it up. Firstly, the research quantifies only holdings by Johannesburg Stock Exchange (JSE)-listed company directors of JSE-listed company shares and therefore excludes their wealth in other asset classes. Secondly, it only shows one side of the balance which excludes any debt still owing on the purchase of those shares. Thirdly, it excludes the wealth of private company directors. Within these limitations however, the results we obtained are quantifiable and meaningful.

Who Owns Whom conducted wealth research for the *Financial Mail* in the 1990s which stopped with a change of editorship at that publication. We were approached to revive this research in 2007 by then *Business Times* editor, Marcia Klein, and *Sunday Times* editor, Mondli Makhanya. In the initial years we came under considerable pressure from business and particularly the Business Leadership South Africa (BLSA) for publishing this research. Yet, we resisted as the information was already in the public domain and the research result were real and verifiable. Our work has since become an accepted and expected *Sunday Times* annual supplement.

In the graphs and discussion below, we give the reader an opportunity to witness the vast inequality that defines South African society.

Unpacking the statistics: Figures from the JSE

In 2017, the total value of the top 200 holdings of JSE-listed directors (R450bn) represented 3% of the JSE and market capitalisation. By way of comparison, the top 200 holdings make up 27% of the Namibian market.

Figure 4.1: Top 200 value comparison: South Africa and Namibia

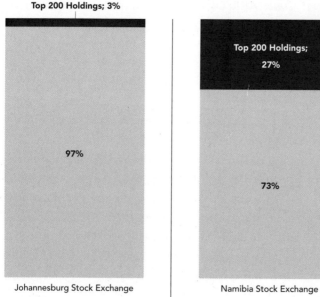

Top 200 Holdings; 3%

Top 200 Holdings; 27%

97%

73%

Johannesburg Stock Exchange

Namibia Stock Exchange

This same total exceeds the entire market of all but three of the remaining 17 African stock exchanges. It is interesting to note that while the Nigerian and Egyptian economies have both overtaken South Africa's in terms of GDP, the JSE market capitalisation is 17 times larger than that of the Lagos and 30 times that of Cairo.

Figure 4.2: Comparison of Top 200 JSE holdings vs African exchanges market cap

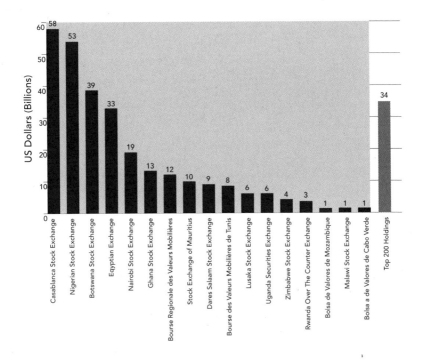

The rich individuals

The highest value holding of a JSE director rests with Christo Wiese. Wiese's value on its own is greater than the market capitalisation of eight African exchanges.

Figure 4.3: Comparison of Christo Wiese vs African exchanges (excluding Top 2)

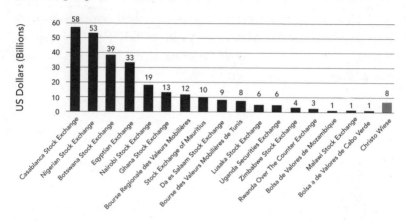

The percentage value of the Top 10 holdings versus the Top 200 was 56% in 2007. This had grown to 62% in 2017 indicating a migration of wealth from the rich to the superrich over this period.

Figure 4.4: Concentration analysis: Top 10 holdings against Top 200 holdings (R billions)

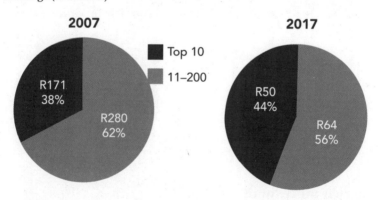

The holdings by the Top 10 totalled R64bn in 2007 and R280bn in 2017. However, it is important to note that these are in nominal and not real terms. The Oppenheimers, Venters and Ackermans do not reappear in 2017 – the Oppenheimers have exited their listed holdings, the Venter empire is a shadow of its former self and Pick n Pay is no longer the dominant retailer in South Africa.

Christo Wiese, Patrice Motsepe, Johann Rupert, Bruno Steinhoff and Laurie Dippenaar have all maintained their places in the Top 10 over the ten years between 2007 and 2017 (Christo Wiese's holdings were calculated before the collapse of Steinhoff.). Newcomers are Koos Bekker in media, Jannie Mouton in education and finance, Stephen Saad in pharmaceuticals and Ivan Glasenberg in commodities.[2]

Figure 4.5: Top 10 holdings comparison – 2007 vs 2017

2007			2017		
1	Nicky Oppenheimer	R16.1bn	1	Christo Wiese	R100.3bn
2	Patrice Motseppe	R13.5bn	2	Ivan Glasenberg	R63.7bn
3	Rupert Beleggings (Pty) Ltd (holding vehicle for the Rupert family interests)	R8.3bn	3	Patrice Motsepe	R19.3bn
4	Bill Venter	R4.2bn	4	John Whittaker	R16.9bn
5	Giovanni Ravazzotti	R4.1bn	5	Johann Rupert	R16.1bn
6	Ackerman Family Trust	R3.7bn	6	Stephen Saad	R15.2bn
7	Bruno Steinhoff	R3.7bn	7	Jannie Mouton	R12.7bn
8	Laurie Dippenaar	R3.4bn	8	Bruno Steinhoff	R12.6bn
9	Chriso Wiese	R3.3bn	9	Laurie Dippenaar	R12.3bn
10	GT Ferreira	R3.1bn	10	Koos Bekker	R10.9bn
	R64bn			**R280bn**	

---

2   When calculating earnings, gains of shares are included. We have attracted criticism for doing so but it is our firm belief that this represents remuneration.

An interesting trend is that the top five earners in 2007 worked for three mining and two construction companies. By contrast, of the big earners in 2015 three are employed by a luxury goods manufacturer (Richemont), one by a financial services company (Investec) and one by a cigarette manufacturer (BAT).

Figure 4.6: Top 10 remuneration comparison – 2007 vs 2015

2015			2005		
1	Bernard Fornas	R103.1m	1	Chris Lynch	R105.9m
2	Richard Lepeu	R95.6m	2	Brian Bruce	R99.2m
3	Hendrik du Toit	R86.1m	3	Roger Rees	R60.9m
4	Nicandro Durante	R81.4m	4	Chip Goodyear	R55.8m
5	Gary Saage	R73.1m	5	Bobby Godsell	R54.2m
6	Markus Jooste	R63.3m	6	Stephen Koseff	R52.4m
7	Ben Stevens	R61.1m	7	Bernard Kantor	R51.9m
8	Bruce Hemphill	R58.9m	8	André de Nysschen	R49.3m
9	Mark Cutifani	R52.3m	9	Glynn Burger	R43.9m
10	Whitey Basson	R50.1m	10	Graham Mackay	R39.3m
	R725m			R612.8m	

The average earnings of the Top 200 was R16.6m in 2007 and R20.8m in 2015. The percentage portion of those earnings by the Top 10 is not as concentrated as that in the wealth concentration analysis graph above. This indicates a relatively narrower spread of earnings across the Top 200 earners.

Figure 4.7: Average earnings of Top 200: Comparison of 2007 and 2015

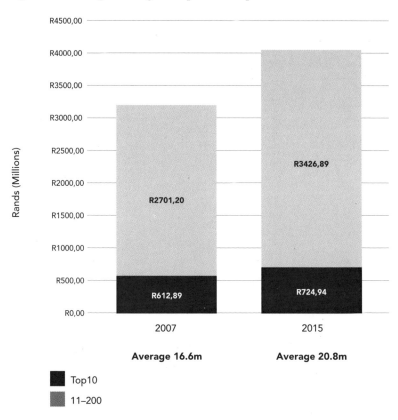

However, this contrasts quite dramatically when comparing those earnings against the minimum wage. The earnings by each director of the top 200 is equivalent to 494 minimum wage jobs using the legislated minimum wage and 138 jobs when using the minimum wage proposed by AMCU.[3]

---

3   The authors refer to the legislated minimum wage in 2017 of R3500 per month. AMCU's proposal at that time was R12 500 per month.

Figure 4.8: Minimum wage to top earnings

	2015
Average	R20,759,125.05
Minimum Wage (R3500)	494
Proposed Minimum Wage (R12,500)	138

On that note, revealing the stark difference in earnings between South Africa's rich and the rest, I rest our collective case.

TACKLING WAGE INEQUALITY: PAY RATIOS AND CAPPING PAY

David Francis and Kaylan Massie

Introduction

THE PROBLEM OF INEQUALITY IS GARNERING increased attention, and for good reason, considering inequality is an intractable problem globally and in South Africa. In the most recent report on poverty and inequality by Statistics South Africa (2017), there appears to have been very little improvement in the levels of inequality in South Africa in the last decade. Inequality, in both income and wealth, remain stubbornly high and this has negative consequences on the general populous' access to resources, assets and opportunities. In 2015, the top 10% of full-time South African employees took home, on average, 82 times more than the bottom 10%, with the average earnings for white workers more than three times higher than for African workers (Isaacs, 2016).

In their recent seminal work, Wilkinson and Pickett (2009) describe unequal societies as 'dysfunctional'. There is overwhelming evidence to suggest that unequal societies are more violent, slower growing and less content than their more equal counterparts. Indeed, inequality, taking various forms, is likely the most damaging socio-economic problem facing South Africa. There is rampant racial and gender inequality; inequality in wealth, access to services, education and life expectancy; and in the life chances and opportunities of people across the country. This essay is concerned with the issue of wage inequality – a particular form of inequality that has very deep historical roots and, arguably, the most drastic economic and social repercussions.

The recent introduction of a national minimum wage in South Africa should be celebrated. It is an important intervention that will improve the lives of millions of low-paid workers in South Africa and it is a good example of the necessity of well-considered labour market interventions. The focus, however, on the lower-wage section of the labour market should not distract us from examining other areas of the wage distribution and there needs to be a broader discussion about policy options to address inequalities arising from pay dynamics at the upper end of the labour market.

This essay focuses on wage inequality, as one of the most important components of income inequality, which, as will be shown below, is the single largest driver of inequality in South Africa. The essay begins by outlining the scope of such inequality in South Africa, with a particular focus on executive pay and the relationship between executive pay and low pay – the pay ratio. The paper then goes on to review international approaches to reducing wage inequality through the use of pay ratios or pay caps. These examples are used to propose particular policy options for South Africa, keeping in mind the important social and economic differences that distinguish South Africa. In particular, it focuses on the power of Section 27 of the Employment Equity Act to achieve substantive progress in addressing wage inequality, if it is properly implemented. This constitutes the first in a series of papers on wage inequality, each of which will tackle different approaches to reducing wage inequality.

Wage inequality in South Africa

An overview

Inequality in South Africa is not an exclusively contemporary phenomenon but rather stretches back for decades, and even centuries (Giliomee, 2003). Despite the democratic transition in 1994, South Africa has made little progress in addressing this, even compared to some of its peers, such as Thailand, Malaysia and several countries in South America. According to the OECD (2011), while some developing countries have achieved significant successes in reducing inequality between 1990 and 2010, China, India, Russia and South Africa have all seen widening inequality, despite the fact that these countries experienced periods of strong economic growth over this time.

A number of characteristics of the South African labour market help to explain this. Persistently high levels of unemployment – which have endured throughout the post-apartheid period – play an important role. In 1994, the narrow unemployment rate was 20%, rising to 26.7% in 2000 and falling to 22.5% in 2007 (International Labour Organisation, 2017). The rise in unemployment in the wake of the global financial crisis is shown in Table 5.1. While there has been some degree of economic recovery, it is clear that unemployment has worsened over this time, from 22.5% in 2008 to 27.7% in 2017. According to the expanded definition, which includes potential workers who have given up looking for work, unemployment has risen from 29.7% in 2008 to 36.4% in 2017.

Table 5.1: Unemployment in South Africa

Indicator (%)	2008	2009	2010	2011	2012	2013	2014	2015	2016	2017
Unemployment Rate (narrow)	22.50	23.70	24.90	24.80	24.90	24.70	25.10	25.30	26.70	27.70

Source: Stats SA (2016, 2017)

These figures, as dire as they are, obscure a highly skewed employment distribution, which is illuminated in Table 5.2. Joblessness is extremely high amongst the poorest 20% (quintile 1) of households, reaching approximately 66% in 2015. The wages of the other third in this quintile who are working are extremely low, on average R1,017. On a per capita basis, quintile one households have an income of R323 per month, compared to R1,491 for quintile three (classified as non-poor) and R12,509 for the richest quintile, quintile five.

Table 5.2: Household indicators 2012 (2012 prices)

	Poor		Non-Poor			All
	Quintile 1	Quintile 2	Quintile 3	Quintile 4	Quintile 5	
Labour Market Participation 2015						
Employed	15.9%	35.9%	52.5%	65.3%	75.0%	44.4%
Unemployed (strict)	25.1%	17.4%	12.3%	9.0%	2.6%	14.9%
Unemployed (discouraged)	5.5%	4.5%	2.2%	1.7%	1.2%	3.4%
Narrow Unemployment Rate	61.2%	32.7%	10.9%	12.1%	3.3%	25.1%
Broad Unemployment Rate	65.8%	37.9%	21.7%	14.1%	4.8%	29.1%
Wages and Labour Market Linkages						
Average Wage of Employed Persons	R1 017	R1 707	R2 651	R4 751	R13 458	R5 787
% Working Households	36.2%	65.8%	71.1%	85.8%	87.8%	69.3%
Average Monthly Household Income	R1 671	R3 125	R4 146	R7 317	R24 090	R8 018
Average Monthly Per Capita Income	R323	R773	R1 491	R3 117	R12 509	R3 611

Sources: National Income Dynamics Study Wave 3 DPRU (2016).
Note: All figures weighted using calibrated weights.

38

The implications of this are quite clear: South Africa must address its extremely high levels of unemployment. But this alone is not enough; these data show that the country has a pervasive problem of very low pay, and very high wage and income inequality, and this issue requires urgent policy attention in order to redress these massive disparities between quintiles.

This is illustrated by the fact that while average wages in the economy have increased since the end of apartheid, and in particular since 2000, driven by wage increases amongst higher-income earners, the real median wage (the wage in the mid-point of the wage-earning scale) has seen little growth and remains well below the average wage. Work by Finn (2015) shows that, adjusting for full-time equivalents, the average wage in 2015 was R9,690 compared to a median wage of R3,784.

The data suggest that wage inequality in South Africa has actually deepened over the last 20 years. In his review of earnings trends in South Africa from 1993–2011, Wittenberg notes that while real wages have risen since 1994, the average wage has pulled away from the median wage, resulting in a notable rise in inequality (Wittenberg, 2017). When discussing inequality, it is therefore important to assess the gap between low or median earners and high earners, rather than using the average wage as a benchmark.

Wage inequality matters, because, as found by Finn (2015), it is the largest determinant of overall income inequality by a significant margin. As shown in Table 5.3, wages account for 90.65% of total income inequality in South Africa – far in excess of the contribution to inequality from remittances and investment income combined.

Table 5.3: Components of income inequality in South Africa

	Absolute contribution	Relative contribution
Wages	0.6	90.65%
Government Grants	-0.01	-1.04%
Remittances	0.06	8.53%
Investment	0.01	1.87%
Total	0.66	100%

Source: Finn, 2015

The distribution of pay is also highly unequal along gendered lines with very wide discrepancies. Furthermore, the bottom of income distribution is dominated by low-paid precarious work, a disproportionate share of which is done by women. Bosch (2015) finds that the gender pay gap in South Africa is estimated to be between 15–17%. The gap in this case is defined as the difference in pay for individuals with equivalent skills and experience doing the same job. This difference means that, on average, a woman must work two additional months to earn the same salary that a man with the same skills and experience would earn in one year. Another report (BusinessTech, 2016) found that white male professionals earned up to 42% more than white women according to median earnings. There is only one women CEO in the top 40 companies listed on the JSE (PwC, 2017).

There are also significant racial pay disparities. A 2016 report, surveying 692,704 individuals, found striking differences in the pay. The report (BusinessTech, 2016), found that white male workers in the formal sector earned a median salary of R21,700 per month, compared to R13,331 for white female workers, R3,612 for black men and R2,887 for black women.

Executive pay in South Africa

Given these dynamics, an assessment of pay at the upper end of the pay scale, and the gap between those at the top and bottom, is crucial. This should be viewed in the context of relative pay for executives in South Africa being amongst the highest in the world, with levels of executive remuneration far exceeding those in comparative developing countries, when adjusted for purchasing power.

Massie et al (2014) note that the problem of perceived 'excessive' executive pay is endemic in South Africa. They cite work by the Labour Research Services (LRS), surveying 296 executive directors in 83 companies across 14 sectors, which found that in 2012 the average annual remuneration for an executive director was R7.7 million. This means that, in the wages of that year, a low-wage worker would have to work for 267 years to earn what the average CEO was paid in 2012. Furthermore, they note that there is little chance that this problem will correct itself. As Massie et al note:

> *At the current rate of CEO pay increases and LTIP (long-term incentive payments) grants, there is no chance that, without meaningful intervention, the wage differentials in South Africa will actually decrease. It will take a conscious effort on the part of companies to actually reduce CEO pay packages or at least stop increasing these packages in order for the wage gap to narrow. Symbolic attempts to grant a 2% higher increase to the lowest paid while still raising the pay for the highest paid will not move this country any closer to a system that is fair to all* (2014: 28).

This has been borne out by subsequent reports from PwC which show that executive pay ratios have remained at up to 62:1 by 2017, showing no improvement from 2015 (PwC, 2017).

Assessing executive pay and pay gaps in South Africa

Executive pay can be compared across companies, sectors or countries in absolute monetary terms. Comparing across countries can be done at market exchange rates or using a purchasing power parity conversion – as in the example below – which takes into account the different costs of goods and services in different countries.

One way to assess the relative level of pay, and pay disparities, is via a pay ratio. A pay ratio is a calculation of the difference between what one employee (or group of employees) and another employee (or group of employees) earns. Pay ratios provide information on how pay is distributed across a workforce. For example, a CEO to median employee pay ratio of 20:1 means that the CEO earns twenty times the median employee's pay. Pay ratio calculations can include or exclude pensions, share incentives, health benefits and other perks. They can also include or exclude interns, part-time workers, temporary workers, contractors and foreign and overseas workers.[4]

When one examines pay data and related measures of pay inequality – such as the pay gap – in South Africa, one is confronted with a variety of statistics covering a broad range of measures of inequality, as illustrated in the tables below. A key reason for this is that it is extremely difficult to get company-level information on exact pay figures, both for executives and for other workers, and especially not on a sector-wide or economy-wide basis. While for listed companies, executive pay is disclosed, it is not always done so

---

4   Some examples include: the ratio between the pay of the highest-paid employee and the lowest-paid employee; the ratio of the top 5% of earners to the bottom 5% of earners; the inter-decile income share ratio, which measures the share of income received by the top 10% divided by the share of income received by the bottom 10%; the 90/10 ratio, which measures the ratio of income of the 90th percentile to that of the 10th percentile. The ratio between different categories of workers could be compared, for example, the ratio of pay between skilled and non-skilled workers or managerial and non-managerial workers; or the ratio between the CEO's total guaranteed package and the average income of the lowest-paid band of workers (PwC, 2013).

in a manner that is accessible, as it often comprises a basic salary, long and short-term incentives, and share options, among others. For other workers, individual salaries are of course not disclosed. Therefore, the figures used in this paper are based on a variety of methods.

Executive pay and pay ratios in South Africa

Adjusted for spending power, high-earning workers in South Africa are some of the best-paid employees in the world – a fact somewhat inconsistent with our status as an emerging market economy. According to 2016 research by Bloomberg, South African CEOs were the seventh-best paid executives globally in that year, when adjusted for spending power.

Table 5.4 provides some comparative figures for pay ratios between 25 countries around the world. Here, the pay ratio is calculated by comparing the average CEO income to the average per capital income in the country (adjusted for spending power across countries).[5] From this table, it is clear that South African executives earn far above the per capita share of national income – an average 541 times more. In India, this figure is 483 times and in Malaysia – a country comparable with South Africa in many ways – it is 66 times.

Price Waterhouse Coopers calculates the Gini coefficient of income for employed South Africans at 0.43 in 2015, 2016 and 2017 (PwC, 2017). This indicates a very high level of income inequality. However, it is lower than the Gini estimated from survey data which was 0.68 for income inequality in 2015 (including the unemployed) and 0.60 for wage inequality (including only wage earners) in the same year (Finn, 2015). What is lacking from the above are trends for intra-firm income inequality. How does executive pay in a given firm compare to the average wage at that

---

5   This is, however, an imperfect measure as the per capita GDP figure takes the overall national income and divides it equally amongst the population.

Table 5.4: The pay gap – a global comparison

Rank	Economy	Pay Ratio[6]	CEO Pay $ Million, Latest Filing	GDP p.c PPP 2015/16
1	South Africa	541.4	$7.14	$13 194
2	India	483.06	$3.10	$6 423
3	US	298.98	$16.95	$56 689
4	UK	228.7	$9.61	$43 006
5	Canada	202.98	$9.32	$45 921
6	Switzerland	179.34	$10.58	$59 011
7	Germany	175.65	$8.36	$47 582
8	Spain	172.42	$6.15	$35 656
9	Netherlands	172.32	$8.66	$50 235
10	Israel	11.42	$4.11	$34 444
11	South Korea	113.98	$4.25	$37 280
12	Australia	113.07	$5.45	$48 225
13	Norway	100.99	$6.96	$68 944
14	Denmark	82.07	$3.79	$46 163
15	Sweden	74.95	$3.67	$48 938
16	France	67.65	$2.84	$41 930
17	Hong Kong	66.2	$3.81	$57 487
18	Malaysia	66.03	$1.76 ·	$26 723
19	Singapore	64.89	$5.60	$86 232
20	Japan	62.33	$2.40	$38 518
21	Finland	61.2	$2.54	$41 461
22	Austria	46.57	$2.21	$47 421

6   The pay ratio compares CEO compenstion with per-capita gross domestic product adjusted for purchasing power parity, which shows how much income the average person generates.

23	China	43	$0.64	$14 882
24	Poland	23.94	$0.65	$27 107
25	Thailand	3.94	$0.06	$16 483

Source: Bloomberg[7] and International Monetary Fund

firm, or indeed, the lowest paid in the firm? Drawing from publically available financial reports in 2017, the pay ratio between CEOs and the average employee[8] at the 25 largest companies listed on the JSE is presented in Table 5 below. Using the average wage – calculated by dividing the total disclosed salary bill by the number of employees – is likely to understate the size of the wage gap. This is due to the divergence between average and median salaries, and because these salary bills often exclude wages for outsourced workers, who are among the lowest paid in any company, such as cleaners and security staff.

Nonetheless, the figures are striking. The data presented in Table 5 cover 1.3 million employees in these 25 companies, who together command a total salary bill of R570 billion. The average salary is R589,850 for the general employee, while the average CEO pay is R55.3 million, roughly 95 times larger than the general employee (BusinessTech, 2017a). This, however, hides significant variation across some of South Africa's largest companies. For Shoprite, the pay ratio between its average salary and its CEO is 1,332; ie., the CEO of Shoprite earns 1,332 times the average salary of a Shoprite employee. Ten of these 25 companies have a pay ratio larger than 100.

---

7   The Bloomberg Global CEO Pay Index tracks average CEO compensation at companies that are members of each country's primary equity index, weighted by market capitalisation.
8   Calculated as the total salary bill divided by the number of employees.

Table 5.5: The pay gap in South Africa 2017

Company	CEO Salary	Pay Ratio[9]
Shoprite	R100.1 million	1332
Naspers	R162.4 million*	264
Steinhoff	R88.9 million*	234
British American Tobacco	R126.7 million*	191
Capitec	R35.6 million	183
Mondi	R85.7 million*	172
MTN	R72.2 million	157
Old Mutual	R43.4 million*	150
Anglo American	R70.2 million*	135
Richemont	R122.9 million*	120
AB InBev	R23.4 million*	82
Standard Bank	R44.5 million	79
FirstRand	R42.5 milllion	78
Nedbank	R36.8 million	77
Sasol	R56.4 million	64
Absa	R29.5 million	58
Glencore	R20.2 million*	55
South32	R43.9 million	54
BidCorp	R26.4 million	54
Vodacom	R35.7 million	50
BHP Billiton	R30.0 million	43
Mediclinic International	R18.0 million	28
Aspen Pharmacare	R17.5 million	25
Sanlam	R22.5 million	23
Remgro	R28.0 million	20

Source: Business Tech, 2017a

Note: * indicates salary paid in foreign currency

---

9   CEO to average salary

On aggregate, Preston (2014) found that across the JSE, the ratio of a company's average CEO compensation to the average wage is 73:1 and in 2016, PwC calculated a pay ratio for a sample[10] of South African firms between 13 and 66, and for 2017 this was 13 to 62 (PwC, 2017). These large disparities show no sign of abating, while executive pay has risen in excess of 10% per year since 2009, average wages have risen by less than 8% per annum thus escalating income inequality (Melin & Lu, 2016).

These large pay ratios are also discordant with what the general population consider a fair pay disparity. Kiatpongsan & Norton (2014), from Harvard University, recently examined data from 40 countries including South Africa to compare individuals' estimates of current wage disparities to what they believe to be an 'ideal' pay gap. Of the 3305 survey participants in South Africa (a sample representative of the population), participants estimated that the pay ratio between a CEO and an unskilled worker in 2009 was 17:1 and believed the ideal ratio to be 8:1. Across the 40 countries studied in the survey, the estimated ratio of CEO pay to an unskilled worker's pay was 10:1, while the ideal was approximately 5:1. Somewhat above this level, the oft-quoted management guru Peter Drucker asserted that a ratio of 15:1, 20:1 or 25:1 was the maximum optimal ratio (dependent on firm size) to prevent resentment and falling employee morale (Drucker Institute, 2011). Clearly, the ratios highlighted above are far from South Africans' perceptions of the pay gap, or what they consider an ideal ratio, indicating that steps to reduce these ratios would be welcomed by society in an attempt to redress income inequality.

It is important to note that pay inequality is not limited to the individuals who receive executive pay packages. In general, the

---

10 Information was sourced from the annual reports of 360 actively trading companies listed on the Johannesburg Securities Exchange, which had a total market capitalisation of R14.0 trillion.

South African labour market is bifurcated, with very high salaries for mid-level and senior management while the vast majority of workers earn extremely low wages. Furthermore, given the fact that executives account for a relatively small portion of the workforce, the issue of pay inequality does not always garner the attention it deserves nor should it be limited to a consideration of only those at the very top. While excessive executive pay certainly is a problem, it is itself a symptom of a broken and distorted labour market, one where bargaining power is unequally distributed, to the detriment of low earners, and to the benefit of a few, extremely highly paid individuals.

Pay ratios at South African state-owned entities

As one of the main employers in South Africa, the state has an important role to play in setting wage standards. The government should disclose pay levels and pay ratios within its ranks, actively work to reduce those ratios and ensure that its suppliers and contractors are doing the same. In this regard, it is necessary to look at the pay ratios within the government and within state-owned enterprises (SOEs); some of the latter are shown in Table 5.6 which highlights pay ratios in nine SOEs.

Table 5.6: Pay ratios at South African SOEs, 2017

Company	CEO Salary	Average Per Employee	Pay Ratio
Transnet	R7.4 million	R353 570	21
Rand Water	R5.1 million	R344 710	15
Eskom	R8.9 million	R696 170	13
South African Airways	R5.9 million	R543 810	11
SABC	R3.6 million	R726 240	5
Telkom	R2.6 million	R535 860	5
Broadband Infraco	R2.7 million	R677 480	4
SA Post Office	R538 000	R161 280	3
Sentech	R1.2 million	R683 260	2

Source: Business Tech, 2017b

It is clear from these figures that the pay gap at South African SOEs is significantly more moderate than in the private sector, with the highest pay gap of 21:1 at Transnet, compared to 1,332:1 at Shoprite. However, these figures almost certainly exclude outsourced workers, such as cleaning and security, and other low-paid contract work. If these are included, the pay ratios would be significantly higher. Calculating pay ratios within government departments themselves is complicated. While national and provincial governments pay according to a salary scale, local governments have more flexibility to set salaries, and thus it is not possible to generate a single set of figures for the government pay ratio.

Policy option 1: Disclosing pay ratios

There are many different options for tackling the pay inequality that has been starkly outlined above. This essay focuses on two of these – the disclosure of pay disparities and the setting of (mandatory or voluntary) pay ratios or caps – by examining the mechanics, benefits and disadvantages, and practicalities of implementation in South Africa.

In order for appropriate action to be taken regarding wage inequality, it is most important to be armed with appropriate and accurate information regarding pay differentials. While the South African pay ratios highlighted above are striking, they are not a complete picture, as they focus on listed companies. A policy for equitable pay needs to apply to all firms, and thus information on pay differentials is required.

International experience

There are only a handful of countries requiring companies, by legislation, to disclose information related to pay ratios. Since 2015, public companies in India have been required to disclose the ratio of the remuneration of each director to that of the median employee's remuneration as well as the average increase in employee remuneration compared to that of key management personnel and explain the difference in this pay gap (InGovern Research Services, 2015). The United Kingdom, similarly, requires companies to compare and disclose the percent change in CEO pay to that of employees of the company (UK Government, 2013. This calculation does not include equity-based pay and companies are permitted to choose their employee comparator group.

In South Korea, annual reports are required to provide information on average employee pay and the pay of top executives, giving enough information to allow investors to calculate a pay ratio on their own (Shin et al, 2015). Starting in 2018, public companies in the United States will also be required to publish the ratio of the total annual compensation of the CEO to the median compensation of all the firm's employees (SEC, 2015). Companies may select their own reasonable method for choosing the median employee and calculating that employee's compensation.

Challenges regarding disclosing pay ratios

There are three main challenges raised by companies over requiring pay ratio disclosure. However, each of these can be overcome. One argument is that the calculation is an expensive and time-consuming process (Caulkin, 2015). For instance, CEO pay is complex and difficult to compute and a company's employees may be spread out across the globe and be employed by a variety of subsidiaries that encompass a number of different payroll processes. However, publicly listed companies are already required to compute and disclose the level of CEO pay. Even if such a practice does require some effort, the equity-enhancing benefits for society of such a policy have the potential to outweigh any additional cost to the company in collecting the data.

Another concern is that companies are able to manipulate the pay ratio reported by outsourcing the lowest-paid jobs or turning low-paid workers into contractors or part-time workers. This could be overcome by mandating the inclusion of such workers in pay ratio calculations even if they are outsourced in these ways. This would admittedly add to the expense and complexity of calculating pay ratios, but would provide valuable protection to the most vulnerable workers and ensure companies are not able to manipulate the figures.

A final challenge is that ratios may not be comparable across companies, industries or countries. Similar companies might engage in different calculation processes, resulting in completely different figures. To be meaningful, clear methodological approaches must be defined, for example regarding which employees are to be compared and what parts of their pay must be included. For telling comparisons, all elements of remuneration should be taken into account – not just cash payments. Even if this is done, comparisons between companies should be treated with care, for instance, small companies will likely have lower multiples than large companies.

Similarly, pay ratios in a company which has a majority of low-skilled workers, such as a domestic cleaning company, will be very different to a company with a highly skilled workforce, such as a technology development company. Any concerns a company has in this regard can be outlined in explanatory text alongside the pay ratio, while those concerned with pay ratios are surely able to understand any contextual differences when making comparisons.

South African application

South Africa already has a legislated mechanism for reporting on pay differentials, in the form of section 27 (s27) of the Employment Equity Act (EEA). As Massie et al argue, 'the strongest possibility for providing say on pay through labour market regulation is contained in the EEA provision that requires designated employers to report on 'income differentials' within the organisation. Designated employers include those who employ 50 or more employees, or who earn above a threshold turnover, and public sector employers such as municipalities and organs of state' (2014: 160). As part of these reporting requirements, these employers must report on remuneration[11] and benefits received by employees.

The power of the EEA4 form for providing a well-informed basis upon which to tackle the problem of wage inequality can be seen in Table 5.7. This is an illustrative example of an EEA4 form for a fictional company in the manufacturing sector. It lists the number of employees by skill level, race, and gender, and provides an excellent insight into the distribution of pay in a company.

The first thing to note is that the average annual executive pay is R825,000, while the average annual pay for the lowest-paid workers

---

11 'Remuneration' is defined in the EEA as 'any payment in money or in kind, or both in money and in kind, made or owing to any person in return for that person working for any other person, including the State'. (Massie, Collier & Crotty, 2014: 160)

Table 5.7: An EEA4 form from the manufacturing sector

	Male				Female				Total
	African	Coloured	Indian	White	African	Coloured	Indian	White	
Top Management									
# of employees	-	-	-	3	-	-	-	1	4
Total Pay	R0	R0	R0	R2 700 000	R0	R0	R0	R600 000	R3 300 000
Average Pay				R900 000				R600 000	R825 000
Senior Management									
# of employees	2	-	-	8	-	-	-	-	10
Total Pay	R720 000			R6 500 000	R0	R0	R0	R0	R7 200 000
Average Pay	R360 000			R812 500					R720 000
Professionally qualified and experienced specialists and mid-management									
# of employees	1	-	-	12	-	-	-	1	14
Total Pay	R120 000	R0	R0	R4 500 000	R0	R0	R0	R180 000	R4 800 000
Average Pay	R120 000			R375 000				R180 000	R342 857

	Male				Female				Total
	African	Coloured	Indian	White	African	Coloured	Indian	White	
Skilled technical and academically qualified workers, junior management, supervisors, foremen and superintendents									
# of employees	20	3	-	7	6	1	-	10	47
Total Pay	R3 100 000	R530 000	R0	R1 900 000	R390 000	R80 000	R0	R1 400 000	R7 300 000
Average Pay	R155 000	R176 667		R271 429	R65 000	R80 000		R140 000	R155 319
Semi-skilled and discretionary decison making									
# of employees	39	4	-	11	7	2	-	-	63
Total Pay	R2 000 000	R2 400 000		R600 000	R170 000	R100 000	R0	R0	R5 400 000
Average Pay	R51 282	R600 000		R54 545	R24 286	R50 000			R85 714
Unskilled and defined decision making									
# of employees	4	-	-	-	2	1	-	-	7
Total Pay	R160 000	R0	R0	R0	R90 000	R35 000	R0	R0	R300 000
Average Pay	R40 000				R45 000	R35 000			R42 857

	Male				Female				Total
	African	Coloured	Indian	White	African	Coloured	Indian	White	
Total Permanent									
# of employees	66	7	-	41	15	4	-	12	145
Total Pay	R6 100 000	R2 930 000	R0	R16 200 000	R650 000	R215 000	R0	R2 180 000	R28 300 000
Average Pay	R92 424	R418 571		R395 122	R43 333	R53 750		R181 667	R195 172

is R42,857, giving a pay ratio of 19:1. But the form allows for an examination of other important pay indicators. At the level of top management, for example, men are paid approximately 45% more than women, while in senior management, white male workers are paid 2.26 times more than their African counterparts. In fact, for all skill levels, whites are paid more than other race groups.

It is clear that the EEA4 forms, through s27 of the EEA, provide an opportunity to build a wage policy based on accurate and complete data. In particular, they allow for an examination of both vertical and horizontal pay wage inequality. Thus the insights these forms offer into the wage distribution in South Africa are unparalleled, and the forms should be used as originally intended. The data from these forms should be made publicly available as a step towards ensuring companies comply with the terms of the Act where unacceptable pay differentials are identified.

We further recommend that listed companies must, in their annual reports, provide a series of pay ratios based on a common specification, as done in some other countries. These could include, among others, ratio between the CEO and the lowest paid; the CEO and median; CEO and mean; and the ratio between the highest 10% and lowest 10% of workers. While the EEA4 forms exclude outsourced workers, these pay ratios should include them. The publication of these ratios is important in and of itself, but is necessary to ensure that companies are complying with any specified pay ratio.

In addition to requiring the publication of pay ratios, it is possible to require boards to disclose the annual pay increase for each category of employee. Harrop (2014) explains that this would see boards being required to justify why pay growth at the top may be greater than that at the bottom. Given the large number of workers that earn wages below the poverty line in South Africa, companies could also be required to disclose the number of working poor that they employ. Requiring such disclosure alongside executive pay levels and pay ratios could prompt a consideration of how much executive salaries would need to be reduced in order to bring all of a company's workers above the poverty line. Furthermore, companies could be compelled to publish these remuneration data in their annual reports, providing a summary of ratios for executive pay, as well as those for race and gender comparisons. This also points to the related issue of calculating and disclosing executive pay: guidelines must be developed indicating how executive pay must be calculated and disclosed.

Policy option 2: Regulating pay ratios or capping executive pay

Mandatory disclosure of wage ratios could be accompanied by the stipulation of a target pay ratio, either voluntary or mandatory. If companies fail to achieve these targets over time, the government can enact incentives for achieving these ratios, such as favourable procurement policies or tax incentives. Should companies' voluntary compliance be deemed insufficient, mandatory regulations setting a pay ratio could be instituted. In addition to regulating such pay ratios, a firm cap could be set on executive pay. Legislation could require companies to obtain certification proving that they comply with a mandatory remuneration cap.

International experience

There are a number of examples of countries capping executive pay or establishing a pay ratio limit. South Korea, Egypt, Israel, France, Venezuela, China and Poland have all established a form of executive pay cap, some based on a pay ratio. Firms receiving funds under the financial bailout regulations in the United States and Germany had limits placed on their compensation. In South Korea, laws require shareholders to set a pay cap for all executives and directors at publicly listed companies unless a cap exists under the company's corporate charter. In July 2012, the French government limited salaries at SOEs to 450,000, equivalent to twenty times the average salary of the lowest paid 10% of workers (Ministère De L'Économie et Des Finances, 2012; French Government, 2017). By 2014, the Agence Des Participations De L'État (2014–15) reported that all publicly owned companies in France complied with the pay-cap decree, demonstrating how a salary cap using a pay ratio can be imposed successfully across many companies as a result of the government leveraging its position as shareholder.

Executive pay in Chinese SOEs is capped at either 12 or 30 times average employee pay for the firm, and plans to cut executive pay in SOEs by 50% were introduced in 2015 (Li et al, 2013; Yuzhe, 2014; Leutert, 2016). Chinese officials stated that these policies were unlikely to result in attrition because executives in China obtain job stability and professional development opportunities they would not get elsewhere. However, Hewitt (2015) reported that several top executives in China's banks had already quit as a result of salaries declining by up to 50%.

In 2016, the Israeli government passed a law that provides that executive compensation greater than 2.5 million NIS ($650,000 USD) cannot be awarded by a financial company if this compensation is more than 35 times the lowest salary at the corporation, thus relating a pay cap to a wage ratio (Abudy & Shust, 2016). This cap applies to all compensation and requires the pay of contractors and their employees to be included in determining the lowest salary, removing the incentive to terminate or outsource low-paid positions.

Polish legislation caps pay in local government and in companies where the state holds a majority stake, at six times the average monthly remuneration in the private sector plus a bonus of three times the average monthly remuneration (The European Institute of Public Administration, 2015). The policy also applied to foundations that obtain more than 25% of their annual income from the government. There have, however, been some challenges in implementation, including resignations and the creation of subsidiaries with the sole purpose of gaining more board seats in order to increase their pay beyond the cap, resulting in a huge cost burden to the state which was reportedly more expensive than if the cap had not been imposed at all (Cienski, 2008).

The United States' salary cap on senior executive officers in institutions that received government bailout funds was $500,000 USD with bonuses of top earners capped at one-third of total compensation. Despite these regulations, Anderson et al (2009) found that 20 of the United States' financial institutions that received the most bailout dollars paid their top five executives an average of $32 USD million each because there was no limit on stock awards.

South African application

The intention behind s27 of the Employment Equity Act – given that income differentials are identified as being 'disproportionate[12] – is to compel employers to take remedial action to progressively reduce this differential. One of the most expeditious approaches to regulating income inequality is to substantively enact s27 of the EEA. But as Massie et al (2014) note, the ECC has not been able to obtain the required data analysis on income differentials that would allow it to construct useful benchmarks by sector, that would allow for norms and standards of pay to be developed.

Under the current labour law framework, employees who are unhappy about excessive income differentials have rather limited recourse. When an employer is in contravention of its reporting obligations in terms of section 27 of the EEA

---

12 'On the question of when an income differential is "disproportionate", although the EEA does not define the term, it provides a mechanism for the Minister of Labour to give guidance in this regard.' (Massie et al, 2014: 166)

an employee or a trade union representative may, in terms of section 34 of the EEA, bring the alleged contravention to the attention of a labour inspector, the Director-General of the Department of Labour, or the CEE. Although the labour inspector is empowered by the EEA to enter the workplace and require the disclosure of information on any matter related to employment law, the power of a labour inspector to obtain an undertaking to comply from a designates employer – or to issue a compliance order – does not apply in the case of an employer's failure to comply with section 27 (Massie et al, 2014: 167 –8).

Furthermore, the Employment Conditions Commission (EEC) is tasked by s27(4) of the EEA to research and investigate norms and benchmarks for proportional income differentials, and advise the minister of labour on appropriate measures to reduce disproportionate differentials, but to date the ECC has failed to do this (Helm, 2015). It is not possible to pinpoint where the fault for this lies, and it is premature to condemn the ECC for this failing. The Department of Labour must ensure that the ECC is properly capacitated to perform its functions as required by the legislation and that it receives the necessary political support to do so.

In light of this, we propose the institution of a cap on executive remuneration, at a level to be set by the Minister of Labour on recommendation of the ECC, and a mandated pay ratio between the CEO and the lowest paid, starting at an initial level, for example 50:1, and gradually decreasing on recommendation of the ECC. There is South African precedent for this. Most notably, PPC Ltd CEO Ketso Gordhan took a R1-million salary cut and convinced a number of managers to agree to a pay freeze in order to reduce pay ratios in the company, achieving a top-to-bottom pay ratio of 40:1 in 2014 (Klein & Masote, 2014; PPC Ltd., 2014). But our recommendation is that a single ratio is specified, one that is set at a level that accommodates a range of sectors. Given the extent and persistence of excessive executive pay in South Africa, it is important that the pay cap is mandatory, although it could be accompanied by a phase-in period, as with the minimum wage. This essay has highlighted not only the extent of excessive executive pay, but its relationship to broader problems in the labour market, and this requires decisive action.

Given the data available in the EEA4 forms, it would be possible to set specific pay ratios for different sectors and adjust these according to the specific needs and characteristics of each sector.

In the way of other labour market interventions, such as the National Minimum Wage, a time-specific exemption should be offered to firms that are unable to comply with the wage ratio, provided they offer an implementation plan to achieve the pay ratio over a specified time period. Given the recommendation for a single ratio, it should also be possible for industries as units to apply for this exemption.

Conclusion: Addressing wage inequality in South Africa

It is important to understand that measures to address wage inequality have precedent in South African policy and political processes, and indeed, are reflected in the commitments in the Ekurhuleni Declaration of 2014. The Declaration notes that:

- Wages are the most important component of income for South Africa's working people;
- Income from wages is the main source of ensuring a sustainable livelihood for workers;
- Unemployment and underemployment, including the legacy of low wages, are the biggest causes of poverty and inequality in South Africa; and

- Large pay differentials between executives and low-income workers undermine the prospects for cooperative labour relationship and workplace cohesion. (Nedlac, 2014).

This essay has demonstrated that pay inequality in South Africa is both pervasive and persistent. While this can partly be explained by widespread low pay in the labour market, the evidence suggests that excessive executive pay is a large and growing problem. Using the pay ratio as a measure to understand income inequality shows that, by some measures, South Africa has among the highest levels of pay inequality in the world, far higher, indeed, than some comparative developing countries.

Given the historical and contemporary socio-political context, the determination of wages cannot be left to the market alone, and indeed there is widespread support for intervention in the labour market, as demonstrated in the wide support base for the implementation of a national minimum wage. There are several policy options available to address the problem of income inequality. Two of the most practicable, explored here, are the disclosure of pay ratios, and the implementation of a pay cap through the prescription of pay ratios or the setting of a wage cap.

It is important to note that in South Africa, the legislative mechanisms to achieve this are already in place. The EEA calls for the disclosure to the Department of Labour of pay differentials by designated employers. This information should be published. In terms of remedial action, again the EEA empowers the Minister of Labour to take appropriate steps to address excessive pay differentials. In the South African context, the prescription of specified pay ratio could be the most efficient to implement, given that there is already supportive legislation in the form of s27 of the EEA, which could prove to be a powerful policy tool. However, to date, there has been no substantive enactment of this provision. An immediate step to be taken is the publication of the EEA4 data, which would reveal the extent of income inequality both across and within companies in South Africa. This data can not only be used to implement and enforce a mandatory maximum pay ratio, but would assist unions in collective bargaining, and allow the government to pursue preferential procurement programmes. Furthermore, the ECC must explore the implementation of a mandatory pay cap, in the form of an absolute cap or a maximum pay ratio.

The National Minimum Wage Research Initiative (NMW-RI) is an independent academic research project run by the Corporate Strategy and Industrial Development (CSID) Research Unit in the School of Economic and Business Sciences (SEBS) at the University of the Witwatersrand. It is undertaken in the context of a national dialogue on wage inequality and the potential introduction of a national minimum wage in South Africa. Information on the NMW-RI can be found at www.nationalminimumwage.co.za.

For their editorial input, suggestions and comments, we would like to thank Gilad Isaacs and Michele Capazario of University of the Witwatersrand.

This paper draws extensively, and in some cases reproduces sections, from a comparative international research brief on wage inequality by Kaylan Massie, which can be found here: http://nationalminimumwage.co.za/wp-content/uploads/2018/01/Tackling-wage-inequality-International-experiences-NMW-RI-Final.pdf

We gratefully acknowledge funding for this research received from Friedrich-Ebert-Stiftung (FES). The views and opinions contained in this paper are those of the authors and may not reflect the opinion of FES.

References

Abudy, M. & E. Shust, E. 2016. 'How investors respond to a mandatory maximum CEO-employee pay ratio? Evidence from unique legislation', SSRN Scholarly Paper No. 2848124, Social Science Research Network, Rochester, New York.

Aggour, S. 2016. 'The war of wages: Maximum wages loses the fight', *Daily News Egypt*, 5 April. Available at: http://www.dailynewsegypt.com/2016/04/05/war-wages-maximum-wages-loses-fight/ [Accessed on 9 December 2016].

Anderson, S., J. Cavanagh, C. Collins & S. Pizzigati. 2009. 'America's bailout barons: Taxpayers, high finance and the CEO pay bubble', Institute of Policy Studies, Washington D.C. Available at: http://www.ips-dc.org/wp-content/uploads/2009/09/EE09final.pdf [Accessed on 7 December 2016].

Arnold, M. 2016. 'Fears over impact of cap on bankers' bonuses "unfounded"', *Financial Times*, 30 March. Available at: www.ft.com [Accessed on 27 January 2017].

Benmeleh, Y. 2016. 'Israel's banks fear brain drain after new law limits pay', *Bloomberg Technology*, 6 April. Available at: www.bloomberg.com [Accessed on 9 December 2016].

Bosch, A. 2015. 'Women are still paid less than men in South Africa', *The Conversation*, 11 August. Available at: https://theconversation.com/women-are-still-paid-less-than-men-in-south-african-companies-45782 [Accessed on 6 September 2017].

BusinessTech. 2016. 'Shocking pay differences between black and white professionals in South Africa', *BusinessTech*, 13 July. Available at: https://businesstech.co.za/news/business/129980/shocking-difference-in-pay-between-black-and-white-professionals-in-sa/ [Accessed on 7 September 2017].

BusinessTech. 2017a. 'CEO vs employee salaries in South Africa's 25 biggest companies', *BusinessTech*, 6 August. Available at: https://businesstech.co.za/news/finance/190506/average-employee-vs-ceo-salaries-at-south-africas-25-biggest-companies/ [Accessed on 7 September 2017].

BusinessTech. 2017b. 'CEO vs employee salaries at Eskom, SAA and other state companies', *BusinessTech*, 24 August. Available at: https://businesstech.co.za/news/wealth/194164/ceo-vs-employee-salaries-at-eskom-saa-and-other-state-companies/ [Accessed on 7 September 2017].

Cadman, B., M.E. Carter & L.J. Lynch. 2012. 'Executive compensation restrictions: Do they restrict firms' willingness to participate in TARP?', *Journal of Business Finance & Accounting*, 39(7): 997–1027.

Caulkin, S. 2015. 'Ratios could align top bosses with workforce rather than shareholders', High Centre Pay, London. Available at: http://highpaycentre.org/pubs/thinking-high-and-low-exploring-pay-disparities-in-society [Accessed on 9 December 2017].

Chutel, L. 2016. 'South African CEOs earn over 500 times more than the average worker', *Quarts Africa*, 19 November. Available at: https://qz.com/841172/the-bloomberg-ranking-of-ceo-salaries-shows-that-south-african-executives-earn-the-most-relative-to-the-average-income/ [Accessed on 25 October 2018].

Cienski, J. 2008. 'Privatisation set to slash Poland's state-owned sector', *Financial Times*, 19 May. Available at: www.ft.com [Accessed on 6 December 2016].

DPRU and CSDA. 2016. 'Investigating the feasibility of a national minimum wage for South Africa.'

Drucker Institute, 2011. 'Turning up the heat on CEO pay', Drucker Institute, Claremont, California. Available at: http://www.druckerinstitute.com/2011/02/turning-up-the-heat-on-ceo-pay/ [Accessed on 9 December 2016].

European Institute of Public Administration. 2015. 'The regulation of executive pay in the public and semi-public sector across the European Union', European Institute of Public Administration Maastricht, the Netherlands. Available at: https://kennisopenbaarbestuur.nl/media/254742/eipa-the-regulation-of-executive-pay-across-the-eu-phase-2-annex.pdf [Accessed on 6 December 2016].

Finn, A. 2015. 'A national minimum wage in the context of the South African labour market', National Minimum Wage Research Initiative, Working Paper Series No. 1. Available at: http://nationalminimumwage.co.za/wp-content/uploads/2015/09/NMW-RI-Descriptive-Statistics-Final.pdf

[Accessed on 29 September 2017].

French Government. 2017. Décret no. 2012-915 du 26 Juliet 2012 relatif au contrôle de d'Etat sur les rémunérations des dirigeants d'enterprises publiques. NOR: EFIX1228286D. Version consolidée au 10 mars 2017. Available at: https://www.legifrance.gouv.fr/affichTexte. do?cidTexte=JORFTEXT000026227470&categorieLien= id [Accessed on 10 March 2017].

Giliomee, H. 2003. *The Afrikaner: A Biography of a People*. Charlottesville: University of Virginia Press.

Helm, R. 2015. 'The vertical effect of section 27 of the Employment Equity Act', Institute of Development and Labour Law, University of Cape Town.

Harrop, A. 2014. 'Business short-termism and the new inequality', in J. Williamson, C. Driver & P. Kenway, eds. *Beyond Shareholder Value: The Reasons and Choices for Corporate Governance Reform*. London: Trades Union Congress, pp. 52–5.

Hewitt, D. 2015. 'Top Chinese bank executives quitting as government pay cuts hit home', *International Business Times*, 4 August. Available at: http://www.ibtimes.com/top-chinese-bank-executives-quitting-government-pay-cuts-hit-home-1873582 [Accessed on 9 December 2016].

InGovern Research Services. 2015. 'Pay-ratio disclosure by Nifty companies', InGovern, Banglaore, India. Available at: http://www.ingovern.com/wp-content/uploads/2015/11/Pay-Ratio-Disclosure.pdf [Accessed on 7 December 2016].

International Labour Organisation. 2017. 'ILOSTAT'. Available at: http://www.ilo.org/ilostat/faces/oracle/webcenter/portalapp/pagehierarchy/Page3.jspx?MBI_ID=2&_afrLoop=49571417 12613&_afrWindowMode=0&_afrWindowId=loeqoumvd_1#!% 40%40%3F_afrWindowId%3Dloeqoumvd_1%26_afrLoop%3D 4957141712613%26MBI_ID%3D2%26_afrWindowMode%3D0%26_ adf.ctrl-state%3Dloeqoumvd_33 [Accessed on 2 October 2017].

Isaacs, G. 2016. 'A national minimum wage for South Africa', National Minimum Wage Research Initiative, Summary Report 1, University of the Witwatersrand. Available at: http://nationalminimumwage.co.za/wp-content/uploads/2016/07/NMW-RI-Research-Summary-Web-Final.pdf

[Accessed on 7 September 2017].

Kiatpongsan, S. & M.I. Norton. 2014. 'How much (more) should CEOs make? A universal desire for more equal pay', *Perspectives on Psychological Science*, 9: 587–93.

Kim, W.Y. 2010. 'Market reaction on limiting the executive compensation: Evidence from TARP firms', SSRN Scholarly Paper No. 1553394, Social Science Research Network, Rochester, New York.

Klein, M. & M. Masote. 2014. 'Ketso Gordhan pockets over R21m in a year', *fin24*, 28 December. Available at: www.fin24.com [Accessed on 9 December 2016].

Kleymenova, A. & I. Tuna. 2016. 'Regulation of compensation', The University of Chicago Booth School of Business, Working Paper No. 16-07, SSRN Scholarly Paper No. 2755621, Social Science Research Network, Rochester, New York.

Kumar, S. 2015. 'The big flaw in the SECs CEO pay-ratio rule', *Fortune*, 6 August. Available at: www.fortune.com [Accessed on 9 December 2016].

Leutert, W. 2016. 'Challenges ahead in China's reform of state-owned enterprises', *Asia Policy*, 21: 83–99.

Li, Y., F. Lou, J. Wang & H. Yuan. 2013. 'A survey of executive compensation contracts in China's listed companies', *China Journal of Accounting Research*, 6(3): 211–31.

Lipkin, D. 2016. 'Israeli bankers quit over salary cap', *Global Finance Magazine*, July/August. Available at: https://www.gfmag.com/magazine/julyaugust-2016/israeli-bankers-quit-over-salary-cap [Accessed on 9 December 2016].

Massie, K. 2017. 'Tackling wage inequality: International experiences', National Minimum Wage Research Initiative. Wage Inequality Report No. 1. Available at: http://nationalminimumwage.co.za/wp-content/uploads/2018/01/Tackling-wage-inequality-International-experiences-NMW-RI-Final.pdf [Accessed on 1 December 2017].

Massie, K., D. Collier & A. Crotty. 2014. *Executive Salaries in South Africa: Who Should Have a Say on Pay?* Johannesburg: Jacana Media.

Melin, A. & W. Lu. 2016. 'SA CEOs seventh best paid in the world, says survey', *Business Day*, 17 November. Available at: https://www.businesslive.co.za/bd/economy/2016-11-17-sa-ceos-seventh-best-paid-in-the-world-says-survey/ [Accessed on 7 September 2017].

Ministère De L'Économie et Des Finances. 2012. *The French State as Shareholder.* Available at: http://www.economie.gouv.fr/files/files/directions_services/agence-participations-etat/Documents/Rapports-de-l-Etat-actionnaire/2012/Overview_2012.pdf [Accessed on 25 November 2016].

National Treasury. *Medium Term Budget Policy Statement.* Available at: http://www.treasury.gov.za/documents/national%20budget/2016/review/chapter%202.pdf [Accessed on 7 September 2017].

Nedlac. 2014. 'Declaration of the Labour Relations Indaba (Ekurhuleni Declaration)'. Available at: http://nationalminimumwage.co.za/wpcontent/uploads/2015/08/0012indaba_declaration.pdf [Accessed on 2 October 2017].

OECD, 2011. *The Role of Institutional Investors in Promoting Good Corporate Governance.* Paris, France: OECD Publishing.

Petroff, A. 2016. 'UK could force companies to reveal worker-CEO pay gap', *CNN Money*, 29 November. Available at: http://money.cnn.com/ [Accessed on 1 December 2016].

PPC Ltd., 2014. *PPC People Review.* South Africa: PPC Ltd. Available at: https://www.ppc.co.za/media/101381/PPC-People-Review.pdf [Accessed on 27 January 2017].

Preston, B. 2014. *Executive Remuneration in SA.* South Africa: Mergence Investment Managers. Available at: http://www.mergence.co.za/media/11312/an%20analysis%20of%20executive%20remuneration%20in%20sa%20final.pdf [Accessed on 27 January 2017].

PwC. 2013. *Executive Directors' Remuneration: Practices and Trends Report* (5th edn). South Africa: PwC. Available at: http://www.pwc.co.za/en/publications/executive-directors-report.html [Accessed on 7 December 2016].

PwC. 2017. *Executive directors: Practices and Remuneration Trends Report* (9th edn). South Africa: PwC. Available at: https://www.pwc.co.za/en/assets/pdf/executive-directors-report-2017.pdf [Accessed on 5 September 2017].

Rousseau, N. 2016. 'Salaire des patrons: la limitation rejetée de justesse à l'Asemblée', *Libération*, 26 May. Available at: http://www.liberation.fr/

france/2016/05/26/salaire-des-patrons-la-limitation-rejetee-de-justesse-a-l-assemblee_1455362 [Accessed on 10 March 2017].

Saied, M. 2015. 'Maximum wage law has yet to be applied in Egypt', *Egypt Pulse*, 24 June. Available at: http://www.al-monitor.com/pulse/originals/2015/06/egypt-sisi-maximum-wage-law-banks.html [Accessed on 9 December 2016].

Schäfer, D. 2013. 'Higher bank salaries poised to offset Brussels bonus cap', *Financial Times*, 17 July. Available at: www.ft.com [Accessed on 27 January 2017].

SEC. 2015. Pay ratio disclosure 17 CFR Parts 229 and 249 (5 August 2015). Washington, D.C.: Securities and Exchange Commission. Available at: https://www.sec.gov/rules/final/2015/33-9877.pdf [Accessed on 27 January 2017].

Shin, J.Y., S.C. Kang, J.H. Hyun & B.J. Kim. 2015. 'Determinants and performance effects of executive pay multiples: Evidence from Korea', *ILR Review*, 68(1): 53–78.

Statistics South Africa. 2014. *Poverty Trends in South Africa: An Examination of Absolute Poverty between 2006 and 2011*. Pretoria: Stats SA.

Statistics South Africa. 2016. *Labour Market Dynamics in South Africa, 2015*. Pretoria: Stats SA.

Statistics South Africa. 2017a. *Quarterly Labour Force Survey: Quarter 1, 2017*. Pretoria: Stats SA. Available at: http://www.statssa.gov.za/publications/P0211/P02111stQuarter2017.pdf [Accessed on 7 September 2017].

Statistics South Africa. 2017b. *Poverty Trends in South Africa*. Pretoria: Stats SA. Available at: http://www.statssa.gov.za/publications/Report-03-10-06/Report-03-10-062015.pdf [Accessed on 7 September 2017].

UK Government, 2013. 'Large and medium-sized companies and groups (Accounts and Reports) (Amendment) Regulations 2013, 2013 No. 1981.

US Government. 2009a. *Excessive Pay Shareholder Approval Act*, S. 1006, 111th Cong. (2009).

Wilkinson, R.G. & K. Pickett. 2010. *The Spirit Level: Why Equality Is Better For Everyone*. London: Penguin Books.

World Bank. 2016. *South Africa Economic Update*. Available at: http://

www.worldbank.org/en/country/southafrica/publication/south-africa-economic-update-promoting-faster-growth-poverty-alleviation-through-competition [Accessed on 5 September 2017].

Yuzhe, Z. 2014. 'Gov't again tries trimming the fat by slashing pay of SOE executives', *Caixin Online*, 25 September. Available at: http://english.caixin.com/2014-09-25/100732978.html [Accessed on 14 December 2016].

PART 3

THE STRUCTURAL DIMENSIONS OF INEQUALITY IN SOUTH AFRICA

THE SYSTEMIC UNDERPINNINGS OF INEQUALITY IN SOUTH AFRICA

Neva Seidman Makgetla

Why inequality matters – and why it persists

SOUTH AFRICA RANKS AMONGST THE MOST UNEQUAL economies in the world – at least amongst those countries that publish figures on inequality.[13] In the 2010s, its Gini coefficient, which is a way to compare inequality across countries (the higher the Gini, the greater the inequality) was estimated at between 0.63 and 0.68, depending on the source (Statistics South Africa, 2017: 21; World Bank, 2018). Figure 6.1 illustrates that South Africa was amongst the four highest Gini coefficients recorded in the decade between 2005 and 2015. The other two countries with a Gini coefficient estimated at over 0.60 were Botswana and Namibia.

---

13 Of the total 217 countries included in the World Bank's World Development Indicators, only 131 reported a Gini coefficient for any year in the decade to 2016. Many of the economies that depend on petroleum and other mineral resources, which are likely also highly unequal, do not provide data; others publish figures that appear overly optimistic. For instance, according to the World Bank's World Development database, in 2008 Angola's Gini coefficient was 0.43, which would mean it was almost as equitable as China, Israel and Turkey and far more egalitarian than South Africa.

Figure 6.1: Distribution of Gini coefficients across reporting countries

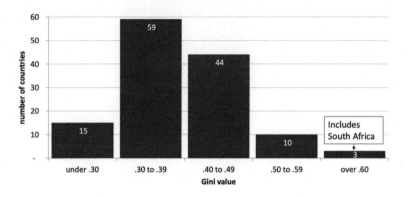

Source: World Bank, 2018

In South Africa, inequality is still largely aligned with race, although a diversity of races can be seen increasing in the rich group. In 2016, 8% of all households were white, but they constituted 47% of the richest 10% of households, and less than 5% of households in the poorest six deciles.

Figure 6.2: Race of household head by income decile, 2016

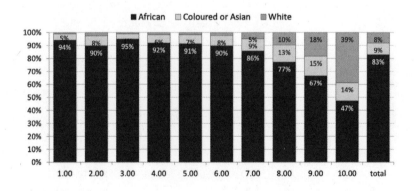

Source: Stats SA, 2017

Inequality has profound economic and political effects. They are particularly strong when it aligns with ethnicity and regions, as in South Africa. Most obviously, high levels of inequality necessarily mean the poverty is more extensive and deeper at a given level of national income. But inequality also fuels conflict over assets and privilege in the form of crime, protests and policy contestation.

Continual conflict between different groups in itself slows growth by making investors more uncertain. As Figure 6.3 shows, over the long run, amongst low- and middle-income countries, the most unequal economies have markedly lower growth rates.

Figure 6.3: Growth in low- and middle-income economies according to Gini level

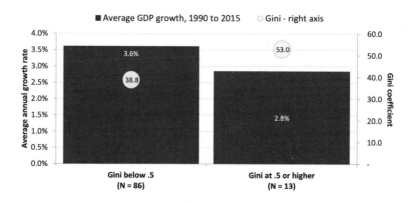

Note: Growth is the average growth rate for the summed GDP of countries in the sample. The Gini for the group is the latest available Gini for each country after 2006, weighted by the share of the country in the summed GDP of the group. China is excluded because its size makes it an outlier; Ukraine is excluded because of the effects of the invasion in 2014.

Source: World Bank, 2018

In South Africa, apartheid entrenched deeply inequitable economic systems based on racial categorisation and gender. A core question for economic policy is why the end of explicitly discriminatory laws and practices from 1994 led to only marginally more equal economic outcomes. In effect, through 2018, the democratic era saw little reduction in overall inequality, although the high-income group became substantially more representative by race and gender.

The rest of this chapter explores the factors behind this situation. It first briefly reviews how apartheid affected the structure of business; access to quality education and residential areas; infrastructure; and the organisation of work, which effectively set up a strong dichotomy between highly skilled and unskilled jobs. It then outlines how the system adapted in the democratic era in ways that maintained fundamental economic inequalities although with somewhat greater racial integration at the top. The final section explores the effects of government programmes in this context.

The historic foundations of inequality in South Africa

South Africa's profound inequality was largely created by state action before 1994, which in effect enriched a minority by holding down economic opportunities and incomes from the majority. The process entrenched systems around access to resources and work organisation that continue to shape decision-making even after apartheid laws were struck from the books.

Economic discrimination under apartheid centred on limiting the access of the majority to education, urban residence and infrastructure as well as ownership of businesses and land. These systems combined with deeply unequal and hierarchical work organisation in most formal enterprises. This section very briefly outlines the economic effects of each of these areas in turn. It then reviews the implications for economic power.

Apartheid systems promoting inequality

In terms of *ownership*, apartheid laws limited black people's rights to own their homes and land in areas designed for 'whites'. A central result of land restrictions, which dated back well before formal apartheid was introduced, was the virtual destruction of most African agriculture. Apartheid legislation also stopped most black-owned businesses from operating in urban centres, and reduced access to credit, especially for African women. In these circumstances, market and government institutions evolved to serve established formal business, but rarely developed facilities to support emerging informal producers, for instance by supplying input, training, finance, accounting services and access to retail outlets.

In *education,* apartheid rules effectively limited access to quality education in order to create a shortage. That, in turn, increased the premium for skills, making it easier for whites, who had privileged access to training and education, to claim 'European' pay and benefits. The earliest official information on education levels is from the 1996 census, because before 1994 the official statistical service did not fully survey Africans even in the census. In 1996, 25% of whites aged from 18 to 64 had a post-secondary degree or diploma, compared to 3% of Africans. As a result, although whites made up just 13% of the population, they accounted for 49% of working-aged people with a post-secondary education or training (see Figure 6.10).

Black *residential rights* were restricted. For most of the apartheid era, Africans could only live legally in urban areas if they had formal employment, which effectively meant working for a formal (white) employer in most cases. People without urban residential rights, and the families of many workers, were compelled to live in the impoverished so-called 'homelands', which were overcrowded in many places, devoid of natural resources and with weak infrastructure at best. Even in the cities, most Africans were not allowed to own housing and were forced to live in townships far from economic centres, making it harder to work or start a business.

The state provided *municipal services* in industrial sites and suburbs restricted to non-Africans that approached the levels found in high-income economies. In contrast, African areas typically lacked running water, electricity, waste removal and adequate roads. In 1996, over 88% of non-Africans had electricity, water in their houses, flush toilets and weekly refuse removal. For Africans, in contrast, access ranged from 27% for piped water to 44% for electricity (see Figure 6.13).

Apartheid encouraged, and in some respects enforced, *workplace organisation* that provided for a relatively few high skilled workers and deskilled, elementary positions for the majority. This organisation of work was most pronounced in the mines and farms. It was linked to highly hierarchical work organisation, where employers could often call on the state to enforce workplace discipline, for instance by using political or residential laws to retaliate against shop stewards.

Economic power under apartheid

Taken together, apartheid systems resulted in low levels of income-generating employment and business ownership and self-employment compared to other upper-middle-income economies. As Figure 6.7 shows, in 1991, around two out of five working-aged people in South Africa were employed, according to ILO estimates, compared to almost three out of five in other upper-middle-income countries excluding China. The disparity was even greater for self-employment, largely because of the suppression of small-scale farming. In 1991, only just over one in 20 South Africans was self-employed, compared to one in five in other upper-middle-income economies, again excluding China.

The flip side of the marginalisation and subordination of the majority in the economy was the concentration of economic power in a relatively small number of powerful conglomerates. These conglomerates were historically rooted in the mining value chain. Mining and refineries mostly require large investments, which, in turn, generally leads to concentrated ownership. In large part because exchange controls and sanctions limited their access to investments outside of South Africa, the mining houses developed extensive holdings in manufacturing and financial institutions.

The apartheid state also directly promoted concentration. Most obviously, it supported white-owned formal business of all kinds, while restricting competition from the majority of the population. The results were most visible in the food value chain, which was dominated by 60,000 well-organised commercial farmers, their marketing co-ops, a few large food processing conglomerates and the formal retail chains.

In addition, the state used its parastatals to support the dominant companies along the mining value chain. To that end, it provided cheap coal-based electricity and dedicated rail and harbour facilities. It also established Sasol and Iscor, both major refineries and mining companies in their own right.

The result of these trends was that by the transition to democracy, the South African economy was unusually concentrated. The strongest companies emerged in mining and refineries, which dominated exports as well as manufacturing production; the financial sector; and the food value chain.

Estimates suggested that at the end of the 1980s, a single mining finance group, Anglo American, controlled over half of the value of listed South African companies. The privatisation of Sasol and Iscor (respectively in the 1970s and 1980s) established near-monopoly refineries in basic steel and chemicals production, arguably increasing the cost of key industrial inputs. Absa, Standard Bank, First National Bank and Nedcor held four-fifths of financial assets. In the state sector, Eskom, Transnet and Telkom owned 16% of the country's fixed capital stock, up from 4% in 1970.

The reproduction of inequality

To understand the reproduction of inequality after apartheid requires an understanding of how the systems that entrenched it under apartheid have evolved since 1994. From this standpoint, inequality persists because of highly concentrated economic power, reinforced by continued inequalities in education, residence, infrastructure and work organisation. In all of these areas, the democratic state introduced reforms, but they did not go far enough to bring about a step change in inequality.

Trends in ownership and investment

The democratic era changed the role of the dominant domestic and foreign investors. Three trends stood out: divestment by the major mining conglomerates, which sold assets to a more diverse group of foreign and local investors; a vast increase in portfolio investment, largely from overseas, which brought an escalation in the value of financial assets; and increased investment by the state-owned companies from around 2003. Despite these shifts, the leading industries in South Africa – particularly along the mining value chain, in banking and retail – remained heavily concentrated, with a few large companies controlling the bulk of production and assets.

In mining, after 1994 the major companies shed most of their non-mining assets as well as less profitable mines in order to pursue mining opportunities in the region and overseas. In effect, they reverted to being international mining firms, with primary listings abroad, rather than South African conglomerates.

In the early 2000s, the largest mining houses sold most of their holdings in the maturing gold mines. When the platinum price dropped from 2012, they began to sell those holdings as well. By 2017, only a third of Anglo American's assets were located in South Africa, compared to almost three quarters in the late 1990s, and it had moved its main listing to London.

The divested mines were generally sold to smaller, more local companies, led by Harmony and Sibanye. Manufacturing assets were generally acquired by foreign companies or by local managers.

The trend was most pronounced in auto and metals refining. The auto industry saw a return of multinational companies that had pulled out of South Africa in the 1980s in response to growing internal resistance and international isolation. In metals refining, in the early 2000s Anglo American sold its shares in Iscor, still South Africa's largest steel producer, to Arcelor Mittal. In addition, in the 1990s, Eskom had an oversupply of electricity, so it worked with the IDC and government to encourage investment in ferro-alloys and aluminium. The result was a set of large new refineries owned primarily by European companies.

The financial industry also underwent substantial changes as the economy opened up after 1994, without becoming less concentrated. It grew rapidly relative to the economy, in large part because South Africa began to attract foreign speculative investment while the retirement funds shifted funds from government bonds into equity. As Figure 6.4 shows, South Africa experienced substantially larger portfolio investment than other upper-middle-income economies, but also less direct investment from abroad.

Figure 6.4: Portfolio and direct capital inflows as percentage of GDP, South Africa compared to other upper-middle-income economies

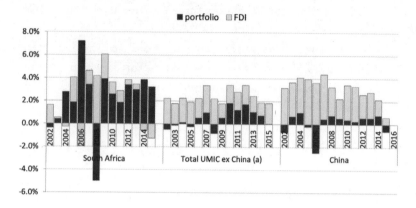

Note: (a) Sample consists of 32 countries.
Source: World Bank, 2018

From 1994 to 2017, the value of equity trades on the stock exchange grew from 10% of the GDP to 136%. That rate of growth relative to the GDP was exceeded only by China, and the 2016 ratio was the fourth highest in the world.

These trends led to significant shifts in the structure of ownership of the stock exchange, as Figure 6.5 shows. Institutions and foreign ownership – both largely retirement funds – substantially increased their share, while Anglo American saw a decline. The institutional investments in part replaced bank management of financial holdings. Black ownership increased when the metals price boom from 2002 to 2011 enabled leveraged buy outs, but declined from 2012, as both mining share prices and profits fell sharply.

Finally, the state-owned companies substantially increased their investment from the early 2000s. In large part, this came about because the commodity boom both increased government revenues, making higher public investments easier to manage, while the mines

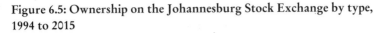

Figure 6.5: Ownership on the Johannesburg Stock Exchange by type, 1994 to 2015

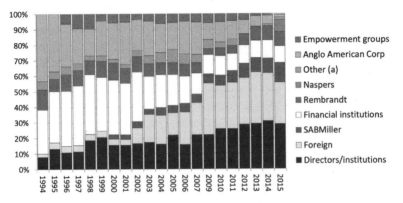

Note: Derived from annual reports publication of leading investors.
Source: Who Owns Whom, 2016

and refineries needed improved electricity as well as expanded bulk transport. As Figure 6.6 shows, the value of the state-owned companies' fixed assets dropped 7% from 1994 to 2003, but then rose some 91% in constant terms by 2016. As a result, these companies increased their share in the national stock of fixed assets from a post-apartheid low of 14% in 2006 to 19% a decade later.

Figure 6.6: Fixed assets owned by state-owned companies, as a percentage of total national fixed assets and an index of value in constant rand (1994 = 100)

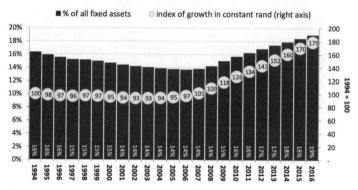

Source: SARB, 2018

Despite these ownership transactions, overall concentration remained high. In 2014, South Africa had over 600 000 formal enterprises, but just 616 of them paid two thirds of all company income tax.

The financial sector saw a significant increase in concentration in the democratic era. From 1994 to 2016, the share of the four largest banks rose from 80% to 88%, while the number of registered banks dropped from 34 to 16. At the same time, bank assets climbed from 60% to 105% of the GDP.

At the other end of the scale, South Africa continued to have substantially lower levels of self-employment than peer economies.

As Figure 6.7 shows, from 1991 to 2016, according to ILO findings based on official South African data, around 6% of all working-aged people in South Africa were self-employed. Outside of China, in contrast, the figure was 19%, which is lower than in 1991, but still well above the South African level. In China, the share of working people in self-employment dropped from 56% to 25% over this period, as urbanisation brought about a rapid decline in farming.

Figure 6.7: Self-employed people as percentage of working-aged population, 1994 and 2016

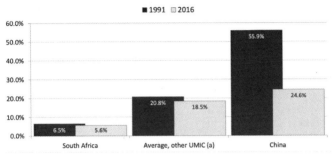

Source: World Bank, 2018

There was little sign of an uptick in the number of smaller businesses, although data are not available for the 1990s. From 2008, the number of formal businesses remained essentially unchanged.

Representation of races in business and, even more, the public sector improved substantially in the democratic era. Still, whites remained significantly over-represented in higher paid and powerful positions, while black women were the most under-represented group. In 2016 the vast majority of both executive and non-executive directors of large listed companies were still white men. According to the downloadable dataset from Who Owns Whom (downloaded in March 2018), three quarters of the chief executives at the 246 large listed companies were white men. Over 800 of the directors were white men, compared to around 200 black men, under 100 black women, and almost 70 white women. According to the labour market surveys, in all formal private enterprise – most of which are small – white-owned firms accounted for 51% in 2015, down from 62% in 2002 and 57% in 2008. The number of white-owned firms fell from 420,000 in 2008 to 360,000 in 2015.[14]

---

14   Calculated from Statistics South Africa. Labour Force Survey and Labour Market Dynamics for relevant years. Electronic databases. Series on sector, type of employment, number of workers and population group. Downloaded from Nesstar facility at www.statssa.gov.za in March 2016.

Figure 6.8: Number of formal and informal employers and self-employed people, 2008 to 2016 (a)

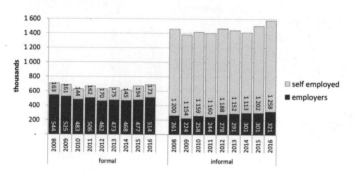

Note: (a) Self-employed here means small businesses with no waged employees. Figures for 2016 are average for the four quarters, since the 2016 LMD had not yet been published as of March 2018.

Source: For 2008 to 2015, calculated from Statistics South Africa. Labour Market Dynamics databases for relevant years. Series on number of employees, main work, type of work and sector. Downloaded from Nesstar facility at www.statssa.gov.za in relevant years. For 2016, calculated from Statistics South Africa. Quarterly Labour Force Survey. Electronic databases for Quarters 1 to 4 for 2016. Series on main work, type of work, number of employees and sector.

Concentrated ownership contributed to inequality in two ways. Most obviously, as Figure 6.9 shows, earnings from businesses were even more unequally distributed than pay for employment. Estimates in 2016 found that the richest 10% of households owned between 85% and 95% of all private assets (Mbewe & Woolard, 2016: 1; Orthofer, 2016: 1). In the richest 10% of households, around one in seven had a business, compared to less than one in 20 for the poorest 60% of households. For the richest decile, self-employment or a business accounted for 40% of total income, compared to around 15% of the (much lower) income of other households.

Figure 6.9: Share in earnings from business by income group, 2015 (a)

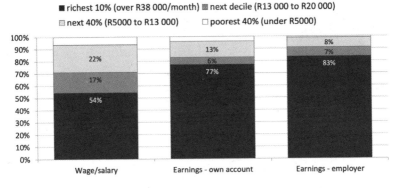

Note: (a) Figures in brackets are the range of total earnings per month for the group.
Source: Stats SA, 2016

The unequal distribution of productive assets also affected economic and political power. In the economy, the dominant companies and farming groups could capture monopoly rents directly, for instance by charging higher prices to downstream enterprises. This was emerged, for instance, in the iron and steel value chain, chemicals and soya production. But they also had substantial power to lobby, sue or use economic pressure on the state, for instance to impose tariffs against cheaper imports – something seen in steel as well as wheat, sugar and poultry. In many cases, different fractions of business had opposing demands on government, most visibly around black economic empowerment requirements as well as tariffs.

Other exclusionary systems

The unusually high concentration of ownership entrenched under apartheid had a central role in maintaining inequality. It was reinforced by other historically exclusionary and inequitable systems. We briefly review each of these in turn.

Education

The democratic era ended the overt racial discrimination between school systems, and reduced the gap in resourcing between schools in rich and poor areas. It vastly increased the share of the population with post-secondary education, as Figure 6.10 shows. Increased education in turn opened access to economic opportunities to a larger group. The share of Africans in all working-aged people with a tertiary education climbed from 39% in 1996 to 63% in 2017.

Figure 6.10: Percentage of people with post-secondary education in total population aged 21 to 64, 1996 and fourth quarter 2017

Despite these gains, the share of the workforce with post-secondary

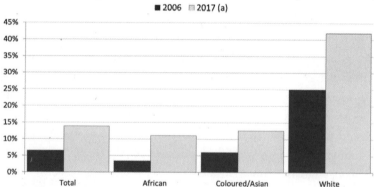

education in South Africa lagged behind other upper-middle-income economies. On average, 25% of the economically active population in these countries has a post-secondary qualification; for South Africa, the equivalent figure in 2013 was just 17%.

The shortage of skills entrenched under apartheid meant that the returns to higher education were unusually high. A good education, and in particular a tertiary degree, remained critical both for getting a job and for higher pay. A person with a degree was 25% more likely to have a job than someone with only a matric qualification. Matric alone increased the chance of employment by 18% compared to those with less education. The median income for employed people with a tertiary degree was R11,000 a month, compared to R3900 for someone with matric and R2000 for a worker with only primary education (Stats SA, 2015).

This outcome was affected by decisions around skilled immigration. In 2016, new regulations on immigration maintained a requirement that in almost all cases foreign skilled workers could be hired only if they would not earn less than a South African counterpart. That requirement effectively promoted existing inequalities by keeping the supply of skilled workers artificially tight.

The education system also reproduced inequality because people from well-off households were still far more likely to obtain a post-secondary qualification than those from lower-income areas. This situation persisted both because of continuing inequalities in basic education and because of the rapid rise in university fees after 1994.

The very different matric results for schools in rich and poor areas underscored the persistence of educational inequality. In 2015, the best-off 15%[15] of schools accounted for 30% of university passes, and only half of matrics got a university exemption. These schools were virtually all in historically white suburbs, where nearby residents had a right to attend and most charged high fees. In contrast, the worst-off 25% of schools, mostly located in former 'homeland' areas, contributed just 15% of university passes. Fewer than one in five of their matrics qualified for university (Department of Basic Education 2016: 53).

Data on the resource gap between schools in rich and poor

---

15 The department of basic education divided schools into 'quintiles' based primarily on the income of their communities and their facilities, but the 'quintiles' were highly uneven, with the top group holding only 15% of schools and the lowest 25%.

areas were not collected consistently, but there are some figures on staffing and facilities. In terms of staffing, the average number of learners per educator in historically black schools, whether rural or urban, was 32 to one in the early 2010s. In historically white schools, the figure was 22 to one (calculated from Department of Basic Education, 2016). In 2011 (the latest data available) almost half of schools did not meet minimum standards for facilities, mostly because of inadequate classrooms. Around a tenth, virtually all in the former 'homelands', had no running water, with a similar figure for electricity. Four out of five formerly white schools had a library, compared to half of other urban schools, and a fifth of schools in the former 'homeland' areas (calculated from Department of Basic Education 2014: 45).

In addition to unequal access to quality education, relatively high fees for university limited access to tertiary education for poor students. Amongst all households with a university student, half paid over R20,000 a year in fees, while most of the rest paid well over R8000 (Stats SA, 2016). Even the lower figure was equal to around a year's income for the poorest 10% of households, although only about two weeks' pay for the top decile. Poor households paid for fees increasingly through loans, which added to their burden of stress and debt.

The reproduction of privilege through the education system is shown by the figures for university attendance by income level. Members of the richest quintile of households accounted for 59% of all university students. In contrast, they constituted just 16% of learners in general education and 22% of those in further education. As Figure 6.11 shows, for every thousand households in the poorest 60%, only around 45 people attended a tertiary institution in 2015. In the richest quintile, the figure was over three times as high, at 155 per thousand households.

Figure 6.11: Number of learners and students per thousand households by income level, 2015

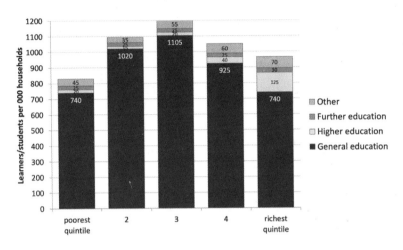

Source: Stats SA, 2016

In sum, the education system continued to reproduce inequality through large differences in access to quality education that linked to location and household income and the continued low level of skills compared to other countries, which maintained a high premium for skilled work, aggravating differentials in earned income.

A more equitable outcome would require a profound restructuring of basic education. In particular, the current centres of excellence – mostly comprising the historically white schools and universities – are highly resource intensive and partly privatised. That in turn makes them unaffordable for low-income learners, while reducing the resources available for other institutions. More equitable outcomes would require either the development of less expensive models for these centres or that admission be less affected by residence near a school and ability to pay.

Geography

The democratic era saw a massive move into the economic centres in Gauteng, Cape Town and some emerging mining towns. Within urban areas themselves, however, the pattern of pushing low-income housing far from economic centres largely persisted.

The former 'homelands'

The former 'homeland' regions remained a pillar of inequality, with far lower levels of income and employment than the rest of the country. The data on the rest of the country looks far more like the norm for upper-middle-income economies on most dimensions of inequality.

The share of the population living in former 'homeland' regions dropped from around half before 1994 to about a third in 2017. In the same period, the population of Johannesburg and Tshwane climbed more than two-thirds; Cape Town, by just under half; and Rustenburg in the platinum belt in the North West, by three-quarters.[16]

Still, income and employment levels remained far lower in the former 'homeland' areas than in the rest of the country. The former 'homeland' regions housed 28% of all households, but only 5% of those in the richest decile. They held 41% of households in the poorest three deciles.

In the former 'homeland' regions, the median household income was R2100 a month, compared to R4050 in other parts of South Africa. Only around one person in four had income-generating employment, compared to around half in the rest of the country. Around a third of 'homeland' households received remittances,

---

16 Calculated from Statistics South Africa. Community Profiles. Electronic database on SuperWEB facility. 1996 Census data on location by area; and Statistics South Africa. Mid-Year Population Estimates. Excel spreadsheet. Series on district council population estimates through 2017. Downloaded from www.statssa.gov.za in March 2018.

compared to under a fifth in the rest of the country, but they averaged only around R1000 a month.

Although the former 'homelands' were nominally rural, almost none of the inhabitants survived from agricultural production. In 2015, although 45% of households in the former 'homeland' regions said they engaged in some agricultural activities (compared to 7% in the rest of the country) only 8% saw farming as the main source of income or food. Most simply did not have the land or other assets to do more. Around 800,000 households in the former 'homelands' owned the land they farmed, but nine out of ten had plots of under 500 square metres.

Because of the low levels of earned income in the former 'homelands', social grants proved particularly important for their residents.

Urban spaces
South African cities remained strongly divided on class grounds, with working-class areas typically segregated from both economic centres and richer suburbs. This situation affected inequality both by making it harder for low-income people to find jobs and commute, and by limiting the value of their homes as assets.

In 2015, more than two out of five families in the poorest 80% who lived in a formal house built after 1996 had received a housing subsidy. Moreover, the share of Africans with formal housing climbed from 53% in 1996 to 76% in 2016 (Stats SA, 2016; Stats SA, 2018c; Stats SA, 2018d). But most new townships were still located far from economic centres, chiefly to take advantage of cheaper land, and the houses were typically even smaller than the traditional matchboxes built in the 1970s. In 2015, the median-sized formal house for the poorest 80% of households consisted of four rooms, including the kitchen and sanitary facilities. In these conditions, the expansion in formal housing generally did not boost economic engagement as much as anticipated.

As Figure 6.12 shows, in 2016 around half of the employed people from the second poorest to the fourth poorest decile commuted more than 30 minutes to work. The figure was substantially lower for the top half of the income distribution, at around 20%. The poorest decile was also more likely to work nearby, presumably because they could not afford to commute.

Figure 6.12: Percentage of employed people in major metros (a) that take more than 30 minutes to get to work, by income decile, 2016

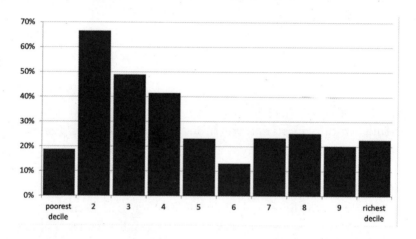

Even controlling for income level, the travel time was slightly higher for people living in RDP or subsidised dwellings than in other housing. That points to the impact of the decision to build most new housing far from industrial centres, mostly to save on land costs and avoid disrupting existing land use in suburbs and city centres.

The persistence of unequal residential areas also affected the use of houses as assets. In 2015, two-thirds of South African households owned their homes. For the poorest 80% of homeowners, however, the median home was worth around R50 000.

The government repeatedly committed to densification.

Ultimately, however, most metro governments focused on improving transport to far-flung working-class neighbourhoods while upgrading city centres in an effort to attract higher-income residents. The national government backed these strategies by providing housing and commuter subsidies. In 2018 alone, it budgeted over R30 billion each for these functions. As in the pre-1994 era, these strategies moderated the cost of apartheid geography for employers and workers, but did not fix the underlying inequalities.

Infrastructure

In line with the original RDP project, the democratic government made improvements in municipal infrastructure a centrepiece of its strategies to address poverty and inequality. Data are not available by income level for 1996, but race provides a proxy. Between 1996 and 2016, the share of African households with electricity climbed from 44% to 88%; with piped water on site, from 47% to 70%; with a flush toilet, from 34% to 60%; and with weekly municipal refuse removal, from 37% to 55% (see Figure 6.13).

Figure 6.13: Share of households with municipal services by race, 1996 and 2016

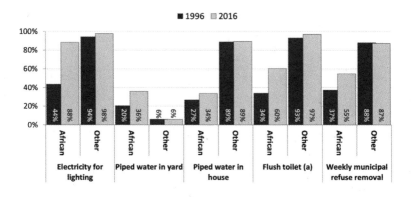

Source: Stats SA, 2018a; Stats SA, 2017a

Stark inequalities in access to municipal infrastructure persisted by income level and location. As Figure 6.14 shows, infrastructure provision was worst for the poorest 40% of the population everywhere and generally poorer in the former 'homeland' areas irrespective of income.

Figure 6.14: Access to municipal infrastructure by income level and geography, 2015

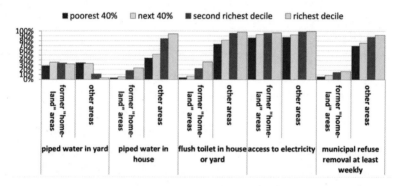

Source: Stats SA, 2016

The failure to provide infrastructure for production of goods and services in most low-income communities also deepened economic inequalities. In most urban townships and informal settlements as well as much of the former 'homeland' regions, there were only limited industrial or well-developed retail sites. Moreover, municipal infrastructure for households in these areas was frequently at a low level and of poor quality, making it difficult to use for production purposes. The RDP argued that improving household infrastructure would permit home-based production as well as raising living standards, but in practice the services provided even in formal townships were not well suited to achieving that aim.

Work organisation

The available information suggests that, while employers and managers have become more representative, work organisation continues to promote profound inequalities in terms of both earned incomes and power.

By a variety of measures, the International Labour Organisation (ILO) found that South Africa had amongst the most unequal system of wages in the world (ILO 2016: 42). In its sample of large upper-middle-income economies, the lowest-paid 50% of workers earned around a quarter of all wages and salaries. In South Africa, they got around half that. In other countries in the sample, the best-paid 1% received less than 10% of all wage income. In South Africa, they got 20%. Not surprisingly, the ILO's summary measure of inequality, the ratio of the 10th decile to the 90th decile of wage earners, was far higher in South Africa than in any of the comparator countries (see Figure 6.15 for more).

Figure 6.15: Share of wage earnings and ratio of 10th to 90th decile of wage earners, selected countries

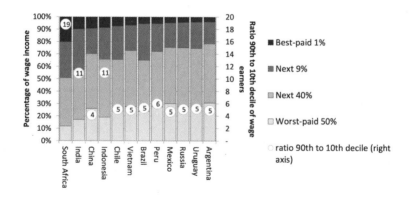

Source: ILO, 2016

Median wages were highly unequal by race and gender (see Figure 6.16). In 2015, the median wage for an African woman was R2500, compared to R3250 for an African man, R10,000 for a white woman and R13,000 for a white man. Inequalities in wages and salaries by race and gender appeared even for people of similar ages and education levels. For employed people, even taking age into account, the median pay for an African woman with a university degree was lower than for a white man with only matric.

A COSATU survey found that in the private sector, perceptions of racial discrimination and abuse remained high in 2012, especially amongst black union members. Some 45% of African union members said their employer discriminated against black people in hiring and promotions, and 38% said their employer abused black people on the job. The figures were significantly lower for Africans who did not belong to unions, and lower still for non-Africans. All groups saw far less discrimination against black people in the public sector.

Figure 6.16: Median monthly wage or salary by race, gender, age group and education, 2015

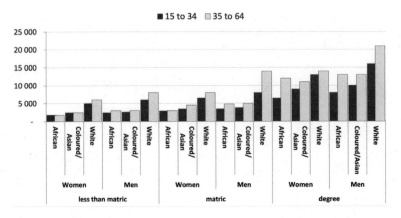

Source: Stats SA, 2015

Figure 6.17: Share of workers reporting discrimination or abuse of black people at work by race and union membership, 2012

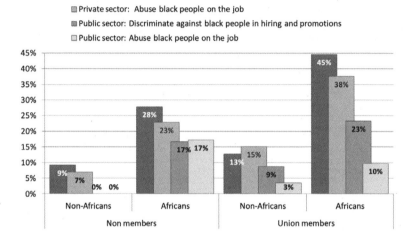

■ Private sector: Discriminate against black people in hiring and promotions
▢ Private sector: Abuse black people on the job
▨ Public sector: Discriminate against black people in hiring and promotions
▢ Public sector: Abuse black people on the job

Source: COSATU, 2012

Perceptions of discrimination and abuse remained widespread in large part because the workplace relations and organisation shaped by apartheid persisted, with the associated unfair inequalities and poor communication. The key elements of the apartheid workplace can be summarised as:

• Poorly trained supervisors with arbitrary decision-making powers and top-down, inconsistent communication.
• Virtually no career mobility or recognition of seniority for black workers, who did not have defined opportunities for promotion, access to qualifications or notches for seniority. As a result, the only way to improve pay for most workers was to win an increase in the overall payscale, which increased the burden on wage negotiations.
• Unequal facilities such as toilets, showers and common rooms for

99

different categories of workers in the same workplace.

• A lack of friendships across levels outside the workplace, in part because different groups lived in different communities.

The democratic state and inequality

The democratic state adopted a number of strategies to address poverty and, to a lesser extent, inequality. This section indicates the main programmes. Taken together, they clearly failed to bring about a radical shift in inequality.

The largest programmes to address inequality entailed various forms of transfers to low-income groups, in cash (through social grants) and kind (infrastructure, housing, health and education). In 2011, according to estimates by Inchauste et al, these redistributive programmes reduced the Gini coefficient from around 0.77 before government taxes and spending to around 0.59, and cut the poverty rate from 46% before state spending to 39% after it. That was a substantially greater improvement in inequality and poverty than seen in peer economies (Inchauste et al, 2015: 31–2).

In 2015, 16 million South Africans, or almost one in three, received some kind of social grant. The maximum old-age pension and disability pensions were pegged at just over R1500 a month in 2015, while the child grant was R350. In 2015, child grants made up 70% of all grants, with old-age pensions and disability grants coming in at 19% and 6% respectively.

In terms of coverage, South Africa's income support programme was amongst the largest of upper-middle-income economies. According to the World Bank's Gender Statistics, almost 35% of South African households received some kind of state transfer, compared to a weighted average of 15% for peer economies. Of course, the other economies had a more equitable primary income distribution to start with.

Social grants accounted for around half of total income for the poorest 40% of households. The impact per quintile in Figure 6.18 is estimated by comparing the average value of grants reported by SASSA with the findings from the General Household Survey on the median income per quintile and the average number of grant recipients.

Figure 6.18: Estimated income from social grants per quintile, as percentage of median income per quintile and in rand, 2015

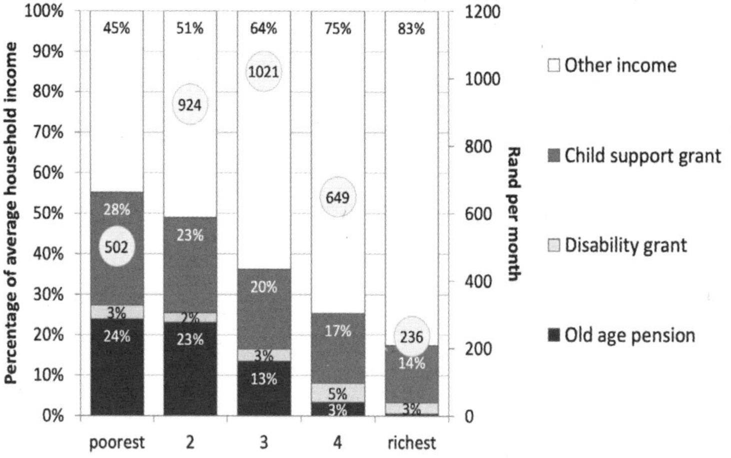

Source: Stats SA, 2016; SASSA, 2016

Both the old-age and disability grants came close to the national and international poverty lines for a couple, while the child support grant would lift half a person out of poverty, using Statistics South Africa's food poverty line.[17] The World Bank's standard of US$1,90 a day indicates similar results.

---

17   In 2015, Statistics South Africa estimated a food poverty line of R501 per person per month in 2011 rand. (Statistics South Africa 2015, p 10) Reflating this figure using CPI, the poverty line would be around R620 a month per person in 2015. By this standard, the old-age pension could support around 2,2 people a month, and the child grant around half a person.

Programmes to transform the economy, which in turn would address the primary cause of inequality, were on a substantially smaller scale.

To manage concentration, the state emphasised competition policy, support for small business, industrial policy, broad based black economic empowerment, and state ownership. All of these policies had some impact, but they were also often poorly aligned and sometimes flatly contradictory. For instance, the Mining Charter incentivised purchases from black-owned companies, even if that meant buying imports rather than local products – which in turn effectively limited job creation and often undermined small local producers.

More generally, support for emerging and small business was on a relatively small scale. This emerged most visibly in terms of land reform, which affected only a small share of the rural population. Moreover, it generally centred on redistribution and representivity amongst commercial farmers, which responded to historic injustice and racial rather than overall economic inequality.

Similarly, the provision of infrastructure and financing for business was effectively weighted towards large, established companies. Infrastructure investment from the start of the commodity boom was largely funded by activities linked to the mining value chain, which tended to influence its location and the types of investments undertaken. For instance, Transnet invested heavily in iron ore and coal lines, while Eskom built large electricity stations that could supply the mines and refineries. While these investments were critical for sustaining economic growth, they imposed an opportunity cost in terms of more decentralised investments that could support smaller producers.

Finally, in terms of labour relations, the democratic state banned overt discrimination, protected union organisation and bargaining, and set minimum conditions for employment. These measures proved inadequate to transform the apartheid workplace, however, although they certainly improved conditions for workers.

In short, in the democratic era relatively little was done to transform economic relationships, in contrast to the very large scale of redistributive programmes. That model proves vulnerable to slower economic growth and the related reduction in fiscal resources. In the event, the slowdown since the end of the mining-price boom in 2011 has had a significant effect on the state's ability to maintain spending on infrastructure, social services and grants.

References

Department of Basic Education. 2014. 'Second detailed indicator report for basic education sector'. Available at: www.education.gov.za [Accessed in November 2016].

Department of Basic Education. 2016. 'National ordinary schools master list, March 2016'. Available at: www.education.gov.za [Accessed in November 2016].

COSATU. 2012. 'Findings of the COSATU Workers' Survey, 2012'. Available at: http://www.cosatu.org.za/docs/reports/2012/final%20 workers%20surveys%20results%20August%202012.pdf [Accessed on 22 October 2018].

Inchauste, G., N. Lusting, M. Maboshe, C. Purfield & I. Woolard. 2015. 'The distributional impact of fiscal policy in South Africa', Policy Research Working Paper 7194, World Bank, Washington, D.C.

International Labour Organisation (ILO). 2016. 'Global Wage Report 2016/17: Wage inequality in the workplace'. Available at: https:// www.ilo.org/wcmsp5/groups/public/---dgreports/---dcomm/---publ/ documents/publication/wcms_537846.pdf [Accessed on 22 October 2018].

Makgetla, N. 2018. 'Inequality in South Africa', in D. Pillay, G. Khadiagala, R. Southall & S. Mosoetsa. eds. 2018. New South African Review 6: The Crisis of Inequality. Johannesburg: Wits University Press.

Mbewe, S. & I. Woolard. 2016. Cross-sectional features of wealth inequality in South Africa: Evidence from the national income dynamics study',

SALDRU Working Paper No. 185/NIDS Discussion Paper 2016/12, University of Cape Town, Cape Town.

Orthofer, A. 2016. 'Wealth inequality in South Africa: Evidence from survey and tax data', REDI3x3 Working paper 15, University of Cape Town, Cape Town.

South African Reserve Bank (SARB). 2018. Series on Fixed Capital Stock: Public Corporations and Total requested in March 2018. Online Statistical Query Facility. Available at: https://www.resbank.co.za/Research/Statistics/Pages/OnlineDownloadFacility.aspx [Accessed in March 2018].

South African Social Security Agency (SASSA). 2016. Annual Report 2015/16. Available at: http://www.sassa.gov.za/index.php/knowledge-centre/annual-reports [Accessed on 12 October 2018].

Statistics South Africa (Stats SA). 2015. 'Labour market dynamics in SouthAfrica'. Available at: https://www.statssa.gov.za/publications/Report-02-11-02/Report-02-11-022015.pdf [Accessed on 22 October 2018].

Statistics South Africa (Stats SA). 2016. 'General Household Survey 2015'. Available at: https://www.statssa.gov.za/publications/P0318/P03182015.pdf [Accessed on 22 October 2018].

Statistics South Africa (Stats SA). 2017a. 'General Household Survey 2016'. Available at: https://www.statssa.gov.za/publications/P0318/P03182016.pdf [Accessed on 20 October 2018].

Statistics South Africa (Stats SA). 2017b. 'Poverty Trends in South Africa'. Available at: https://www.statssa.gov.za/publications/Report-03-10-06/Report-03-10-062015.pdf [Accessed on 20 October 2018].

Statistics South Africa (Stats SA). 2018a. 'Community profiles. Electronic database with census data. Series on education, age and population group for 1996'. Downloaded from SuperWEB facility at www.statssa.gov.za in March 2018.

Statistics South Africa (Stats SA). 2018b. 'Quarterly Labour Force Survey'. Available at: http://www.statssa.gov.za/publications/P0211/P02114thQuarter2017.pdf [Accessed in March 2018].

Statistics South Africa (Stats SA). 2018c. 'Community profiles'. SuperWEB facility. Series for 1996 Census on housing type and population group.

Statistics South Africa (Stats SA). 2018d. 'Community Survey 2016'. Electronic database. Nesstar facility. Downloaded from www.statssa.gov. za [Accessed in March 2018].

WhoOwnsWhom. 2016. 'WOW Datafeed'. Provided by WhoOwnsWhom to author.

World Bank. 2018. 'World Development Indicators'. Available at: www. worldbank.org.za [Accessed on 22 October 2018].

WHITHER A DEMOGRAPHIC DIVIDEND
SOUTH AFRICA: THE OVERTON WINDOW
OF POLITICAL POSSIBILITIES[18]

P.J. Lehohla
Summary by Zunaid Moola[19]

THE CONCEPT OF A DEMOGRAPHIC DIVIDEND is based on the link between a country's demographic profile and its potential for an increase in economic growth. Typically, starting from a position of a high fertility rate and a relatively large young population, if there is a decline in the country's fertility rate over time, there follows an increase in its working-age ratio, which is the population of working age (15–64 years) as a percentage of the total population. There is a corresponding decrease in the dependency ratio (those below 15 and over 64 as a percentage of the total population). On the assumption that there is positive growth in the total population, a higher working-age ratio results in more labour

---

18 The 'Overton Window' refers to the range of accepted ideas in political discourse at a given time.
19 This is an edited, summarised and shortened version of an original Statistics South Africa publication, which can be accessed at: http://www.statssa.gov.za/publications/OP001/OP0012017.pdf. The report was presented at the IFAA Inequality conference in 2017.

resources becoming available to devote to production. In addition, the lower dependency ratio means that, at least in relative terms, less time and energy are diverted away from productive workplace activities to care for the young and the elderly. The resulting boost to economic growth, if it takes place, is known as the demographic dividend.

An increase in the working-age ratio does not lead to a demographic dividend automatically. Rather, it presents an opportunity for higher economic growth, which may be achieved in full or in part or not at all. For the demographic dividend to reach its full potential, favourable socio-economic conditions are required. If socio-economic conditions are unfavourable, a demographic dividend could remain elusive. There is also the danger of a high working-age ratio becoming severely problematic if there is insufficient job creation. High unemployment aggravates poverty and inequality and raises the risk of social unrest.

Demographic change

The experience of many countries has been a long-term decline in mortality rates through the successful treatment and reduction of infectious and contagious diseases. Lower mortality rates tend to be followed by lower fertility rates. If accompanied by appropriate economic and social policies and other supporting factors, this outcome may have a strong, positive effect on economic growth:

> *Because people's economic behavior and needs vary at different stages of life, changes in a country's age structure can have significant effects on its economic performance. Nations with a high proportion of children are likely to devote a high proportion of resources to their care, which tends to depress the pace of economic growth. By contrast, if most of a nation's population falls within the working ages, the added productivity of this*

group can produce a 'demographic dividend' of economic growth, assuming that policies to take advantage of this are in place (Bloom et al, 2003: xi).

The demographic dividend in selected countries in East Asia and Latin America

In 1960, the working-age ratios of six East Asian countries (China, Indonesia, Malaysia, South Korea, Singapore and Thailand) ranged from 51% (Malaysia) to 56% (China and Indonesia). The six countries were chosen partly because they all had working-age ratios between 50% and 60% in 1960, as did South Africa (55%). By 2015 the East Asian range was 67% (Indonesia) to 73% (China and South Korea).

Looking at the long-term increase in working-age ratios in certain Latin American countries and South Africa, we see that the range in 1960 was 50% (Colombia) to 56% (Chile), i.e. similar to the 1960 range in East Asia. Other Latin American countries experienced a demographic transition, though generally not as marked as the East Asian countries, with the Latin American range reaching 64% (Ecuador) to 69% (Brazil) by 2015. The increase was generally higher in the East Asian economies, but the Latin American economies did not lag by much, and, going against the general pattern, one of the highest increases experienced was in Latin America (Colombia) and the lowest was in East Asia (Indonesia). However, the two regions had vastly different experiences in terms of economic growth between 1960 and 2015.

Generally, the East Asian economies achieved impressive growth over a long period. Ahmed et al (2016: 7) say that 'famously, demographic transition in East Asia has been credited with facilitating the region's rapid income growth since the 1960s'. Growth rates in Latin America were much lower, suggesting that a transition to a higher working-age ratio is not a sufficient condition to produce high economic growth. 'A comparison between Asia and Latin America suggests that economic outcomes can differ significantly for broadly similar [demographic] transitions. Asia's more favorable outcomes have been attributed to a stronger focus on human (education and health) and physical capital' (Drummond et al, 2014: 5). South Africa's per capita growth rate from 1961 to 2015 averaged just 1%, which was well below the East Asian growth rates and below five of the six Latin American growth rates. It is necessary for us to consider, therefore, the socio-economic conditions that are supportive of a demographic dividend to understand the variance in growth experienced by South Africa, Latin America and East Asian countries.

Socio-economic conditions in support of a demographic dividend

The socio-economic conditions that raise the prospects for a higher working-age ratio to contribute to higher economic growth are outlined below.

Labour market

As the numbers of working-age people grow, their ability to boost economic growth depends critically on their ability to find productive employment. If a country has high unemployment, its prospects for achieving a demographic dividend are low. An increase in the availability of a productive resource will not have positive growth effects if the additional resources are left unused. High unemployment may be the result of demand-side or supply-side factors or inefficiencies in the labour market. Gender equality is an important aspect of an effective labour market: the potential demographic dividend is weakened if women are denied equal opportunities in the workplace and in society more generally.

Economic growth

A growing workforce needs a growing economy. Without policies that promote economic growth and development, the further boost to growth that can come from demographic transition will be difficult to achieve. Governments can promote long-term economic growth by building strong institutions and avoiding excessive fiscal deficits and high inflation. A stable macroeconomic environment provides individuals with the confidence to save and businesses with the confidence to invest. High savings and investment rates were characteristic of the high-growth East Asian economies during the second half of the 20th century, as were openness to international trade and the promotion of exports. Ahmed et al note the importance of savings and investment in the context of the 'second' demographic dividend:

> The second demographic dividend arises and can continue as countries enter the later stages of the demographic transition. When working-age populations were rising and high, and dependency ratios are low, there is scope for economies to potentially save more, and invest more in both physical and human capital. These additional investments on physical and human capital can lead to a permanent increase in productivity which can persist long after the working- age population shares have begun to decline and populations begin to age (2016: 9).

Developing human capital through investments in social infrastructure (e.g. schools and hospitals) can significantly enhance the demographic dividend, as can investment in economic infrastructure, since reliable and affordable transport, communications, water and power assist exporters and other businesses in becoming internationally competitive.

110

Governance

Macroeconomic stability is one aspect of good governance. 'Macroeconomic stability and low inflation were necessary preconditions for rapid growth in all eight HPAEs [high-performing Asian economies]' (World Bank, 1993: 348). Good governance should extend beyond the economic sphere and should apply across all levels of the public and private sectors.

Education and training

Education and training are fundamental to addressing the supply side of the labour market. If work seekers do not have the skills that employers require, they will struggle to find work. A more skilled workforce is likely to be reflected in the skills profile of the employed, with corresponding higher rates of productivity, remuneration and standards of living. Education facilitates the adoption of new technologies, and educated parents are more likely to have the means to ensure a good education for their children. There is also a crucial role for government. The costs of quality education are high and those who cannot afford it rely on government to provide education services. To the extent that universal education reduces unemployment, quality public-sector education is an important means of reducing economic poverty and inequality.

Healthcare and family planning

To remain productive, workers across the spectrum (low, semi and high skilled) need to remain healthy. Access to affordable healthcare also encourages smaller families, as parents can be confident that their children's medical needs will be met. Successful healthcare outcomes reinforce successful education outcomes. If access to good healthcare is inadequate, the prospects for a demographic dividend are lowered.

Demographic trends in South Africa

Fertility and mortality

South Africa's population grew from 26 million in 1975 to 57 million in 2017. The average annual population growth rate fell from 2.6% in the 1960s and 1970s to 1.5% in 2010 to 2017. The long-term decline in the population growth rate was the outcome of the fertility rate dropping from 6.1 in the early 1960s to 2.4 in 2017. South Africa's infant mortality rate fell from over 80 (deaths per 1,000 live births) in the mid-1970s to 32.8 in 2017.

Population pyramids and the working-age ratio

Population pyramids show the age and gender structure of a country (or community or region) at a point in time. When the fertility rate is high, the pyramid has a wide base, reflecting a relatively high proportion of children. As the fertility rate falls, the base narrows, as was the case in South Africa between 1990 and 2002. The working-age ratio, which is the population aged 15–64 years as a percentage of the total population, increased from 57% in 1990 to 63% in 2002. Between 2002 and 2017 there was a widening of the base of the 'pyramid', but the working-age ratio continued to rise, reaching 65% in 2017.

Socio-economic conditions in South Africa

Labour market

South Africa has a long history of high unemployment. Expanded unemployment includes discouraged workers, i.e. those who are unemployed and who are considered unemployed even though they have not taken active steps to find work. The expanded rate increased from 30% in 2008 to 35% in 2010, partly as a result of job losses caused by the global economic crisis. Thereafter, it stabilised around 35%, but it rose to 36% in 2016 and the number of unemployed continued to grow, reaching 8.9 million in 2016. In each category (skilled, semi-skilled and low-skilled) there was an increase in employment between 2008 and 2016, but the increase was insufficient to absorb the growing numbers of people entering the labour force, leading to the higher unemployment levels described above.

The downward trend in the number of skilled workers during 2014 and 2015 sits uncomfortably in comparison with the NPC's (2012: 157) 2030 vision for 'skilled labour becoming the predominant feature of the labour force'. As a percentage of total employment, skilled employment fell from 25.5% in 2013 to 23.4% in 2016. Inadequate skills are a severe obstacle to job creation.

Economic growth

South Africa's demographic transition and economic growth rates were compared with 12 countries in East Asia and Latin America between 1960 and 2015. South Africa's long-term growth performance was poor by comparison with most of the countries shown. More recently, just prior to the global economic crisis of 2008–09, South Africa's annual real GDP growth exceeded 5% for three consecutive years: 5.3% in 2005, 5.6% in 2006 and 5.4% in 2007. After the slump of 2008–09, annual growth recovered to around 3% in 2010–11, but thereafter weakened again to just 0.3% in 2016. In September 2017, the South African Reserve Bank's forecast of real GDP growth was 0.6% in 2017, 1.2% in 2018 and 1.5% in 2019 (SARB, 2017). The International Monetary Fund has projected annual growth of 1% in 2017, 1.2% in 2018, 1.7% in 2019, and 2.2% in each of the three years 2020–2022 (IMF, 2017).

Recent performance in South Africa's economic growth stands in sharp contrast to the target indicated in the National Development Plan (NDP). The NDP's real GDP growth objective for the period 2011–2030 is an annual average of 5.4%. While that level of growth is close to what we saw in 2005–07, in the current environment it looks remote. As the IMF has noted: 'South Africa has made impressive economic and social progress in the past two decades. Yet, deep-rooted structural problems – infrastructure bottlenecks, skill mismatches, and harmful insider-outsider dynamics – are holding back growth and exacerbating unemployment and inequality' (IMF, 2016).

The NPC's assessment of South Africa's poor economic growth (NPC, 2012: 110) is that the country 'is in a low growth, middle income trap. There are four key features of this trap that serve to reinforce each other. These are:

- Low levels of competition for goods and services
- Large numbers of work seekers who cannot enter the labour market
- Low savings
- A poor skills profile.

South Africa's low rate of saving is all the more concerning in that the 'second' demographic dividend relies on an increase in saving: 'In addition to [a] first dividend based on a productive labor supply, a possible second dividend results from the savings and investments of the bulge cohort as it matures and saves for retirement' (Canning et al, 2015).

Much of South Africa's imperative for growth in the economy and to reap the benefits of demographic change stems from the need to address the country's high levels of poverty and inequality. But high levels of poverty and inequality themselves may be an obstacle to economic growth if there is a risk of political instability. This instability may negatively affect confidence in the economy, savings and investment.

Striking evidence of inequality in South Africa is provided by Stats SA's Living Conditions Survey 2014/15. In the highest-income decile, average annual household income was R689,672; in the lowest-income decile, average annual household income was just R6,279. Social grants play a crucial role in reducing poverty and inequality, but even after taking social grants into account, the difference between rich and poor is vast.

In 2015, 30.4 million individuals, or 55.5% of the population, fell below the upper-bound poverty line of R992 per month (using 2015 prices). Although this was an improvement (i.e. a decrease) compared to 2006, both the number and percentage were up when compared to 2011. Approximately, a quarter of the population fell below the food poverty line (extreme poverty) in 2015, down from 28% in 2006 but up from 21% in 2011.

Governance

Following the achievement of democracy in 1994 and the introduction of a new constitution in 1996, South Africa made great strides forward in governance across the spectrum. However, over time, greed and corruption bubbled away, and spread, and became a storm.

In its analysis of South Africa's thriving corruption, the NPC identifies 'four areas in which policies should be implemented towards an accountable state' (NPC, 2012: 447). These are: building a resilient anti-corruption system; strengthening accountability and responsibility of public servants; creating a transparent, responsive and accountable public service; and strengthening judicial governance and the rule of law.

Allegations of mismanagement at major South African state-owned enterprises (SOEs) have received much media attention both locally and internationally. Provided that they are free of corruption and well managed, SOEs can play a valuable role in economic transformation and development. 'Good corporate governance of state-owned enterprises is critical to achieving growth objectives and efficient infrastructure delivery' (OECD, 2017: 29).

A powerful institution for promoting good governance in South Africa is the office of the public protector, which has powers (in terms of chapter 9 of the country's Constitution) to investigate any conduct in state affairs, or in the public administration in any sphere of government, that is alleged or suspected to be improper or to result in any impropriety or prejudice; to report on that conduct; and to take appropriate remedial action. Two of the public protector's reports that have generated much public interest are the Nkandla and state capture reports. Both reports investigated alleged mismanagement and corruption in national governance entities.

Education and training

The NPC is clear on the importance of human capital: 'The single most important investment any country can make is in its people' (NPC, 2012: 296). However, the NPC's assessment of South Africa's education system reflects the need for major improvements, and National Treasury's Budget Review states (2017: 14): 'Education and skills remain at the heart of the country's employment crisis. The lack of opportunities to enter the workforce to gain experience, coupled with poor school education and limited networks, consigns many young work-seekers to long-term unemployment.' The IMF's comment on South Africa's labour market is that 'improving educational attainment and skills will be crucial' (IMF, 2017).

South Africa's school system is characterised by extreme inequalities, from expensive private-sector schools offering excellent education to no-fee public-sector schools where the quality of education is variable. The NPC states that the 'quality of education for most black children is poor' (NPC, 2012: 48). It found that 'South Africa loses half of every cohort that enters the school system by the end of the 12-year schooling period, wasting significant human potential and harming the life-chances of many young people' (NPC, 2012: 305). Regarding higher education, the NPC states that 'the performance of existing institutions ranges from world-class to mediocre' (NPC, 2012: 50).

The NPC is also critical of the further education and training system, which it found to be 'not effective. It is too small and the output quality is poor. Continuous quality improvement is needed as the system expands (NPC, 2012: 50). Approximately 65% of college students are unable to find work experience... The college sector is intended as a pathway for those who do not follow an academic path, but it suffers from a poor reputation due to the low rate of employment of college graduates' (NPC, 2012: 320).

The OECD finds that the 'biggest challenge in South Africa is the unequal quality of school education, its low average level and high drop-out rates' (2017: 48). It suggests that gaps in South Africa's entrepreneurial skills are partly the result of low-quality education and lack of work experience and that shortages and mismatches of skills are barriers to growth and inclusiveness (OECD, 2017: 10–11).

Healthcare and family planning

Family planning has come a long way since the 1960s and South Africa's fertility rate having declined from 6.1 in the early 1960s to 2.7 in 2008 and 2.4 in 2017. Information on reproductive health is widely available, although more needs to be done to reduce teenage pregnancies. Stats SA's General Household Survey of 2016 reported pregnancy rates (during the year preceding the survey) of 6.5% for females aged 17; 7.1% for females aged 18; and 10.7% for females aged 19. However, as in education, so in healthcare, a minority of South Africans have access to expensive, high-quality services in the private sector and the majority rely on a public-sector healthcare system that is in urgent need of reform.

Structural problems in public-sector healthcare identified in the NHI white paper (Department of Health, 2017: 12–16) include the following:

The inequities and poor quality in the health system are exacerbated by a skewed distribution of key health professionals between the public and private sectors. The main contributor to this inequity is the creation of a two-tier healthcare system where the affluent pool their healthcare funds separately from the poor. The shortage of key health professionals is being experienced in the face of the growth of the population that is dependent on public healthcare services, and the increasing burden of disease among the population, and unpredictable inward migration patterns. This has placed an extraordinary strain on public-sector health services, and on the staff who work in public-sector facilities, thus contributing to the very poor health outcomes of South Africans, particularly for the lowest-income populations and households...

The South African health system is two tiered and fragmented. Almost 50% of Total Health Expenditure (THE) is spent on 16% of the population covered by medical schemes while the other 50% is spent on 84% of the population in the public sector. The population that accesses services in the public sector is usually poor, rural and encumbered with a high burden of disease. Consequently, financial resource allocation and healthcare expenditure is not matching with the needs of the majority of the population...

In search of South Africa's demographic dividend by population group

Four population groups

A legacy of South Africa's racial past is that race remains prominent in socio-economic discourse. Four broad population groups are shown in official statistics, namely black African, coloured, Indian/Asian and white. In 2017 the black African population was 45.66 million, accounting for almost 81% of the total population.

Poverty, income and expenditure

Central to the literature on the demographic dividend is the relationship between demographic transition and GDP. There are no estimates for South Africa's GDP by population group, but comparisons based on poverty, income and expenditure can be made using information from Stats SA's Household Income and Expenditure surveys, while the Quarterly Labour Force Survey contains rich detail on the labour market.

Research findings reveal poverty as extremely low amongst whites (0.4%) and Indians/Asians (1.2%) in 2015, whereas it was much higher amongst coloureds (23.3%) and a staggering 47.1% amongst black Africans. Between 2011 and 2015, poverty decreased among whites and Indians/Asians, whereas it increased amongst coloureds and black Africans.

In 2005–06, average household income was R280,870 in white households (population group of household head) compared with just R37,711 in black African households, a ratio of 7.4. The ratio for expenditure was 6.5 (R198,632 compared with R30,509). By 2014–15 these ratios had fallen to 4.8 (income) and 5.2 (expenditure).

The relatively high growth in black African household income (147%) and expenditure (122%) between 2005–06 and 2014–15 is notable. Is there a demographic dividend to be detected here for black Africans? Probably the two main factors underpinning high black African growth in income and expenditure were a low base and improved opportunities. Following centuries of deprivation and oppression, the era since 1994 has given the non-white population groups opportunities in the public and private sectors of the economy, which were previously unavailable to them. Not only were barriers removed, but black economic empowerment programmes have been actively promoted. Economic and social infrastructure services at municipal, provincial and national levels, for so long heavily skewed in favour of the white population, have been increasingly rolled out to the population at large. With these measures driving catch-up effects, it is difficult to find a demographic dividend effect for black Africans in income and expenditure growth rates that have been higher than those in other population groups, particularly when the racial disparities in levels remain so vast.

Furthermore, despite high expenditure growth, black Africans' expenditure choices are significantly more constrained than those of whites. For example, black Africans devote a relatively high proportion of their household expenditure to necessities such as food and clothing/footwear. Although the proportion (of their total expenditure) that black Africans spent on food fell from 19% in 2005–06 to 15.5% in 2014–15, it remained well above the proportion spent by whites (5.8% in 2015–16). In 2014–15, the proportions for clothing/footwear were 6.7% (black Africans) and 1.9% (whites).

Black Africans spend a high proportion of their budgets on public transport by road (5.4% in 2014–15). For them it is a necessity. Transport is a necessity for other groups as well, but they have more choices, and the line between necessity and luxury (expensive cars) may be blurred.

Black Africans also find themselves at a disadvantage in terms of travelling times between home and work and between home and school. Stats SA's household travel survey of 2013 found that travelling times for black Africans were longer than those for whites, across all forms of travel (train, bus, taxi, car, walking) and for both workers and learners. For example, average travel times (in minutes) for black African workers were 57 (taxi passenger), 50 (car passenger) and 47 (car driver); corresponding times for whites were 55, 34 and 39 minutes. Black African learners had average travel times (in minutes) of 50 (taxi passenger), 39 (car passenger) and 31 (walking); corresponding times for whites were 36, 25 and 16. These findings are the result of most black African homes being located on the periphery of urban areas whereas most white homes are nearer the centre. Comparisons of settlement patterns between the population censuses of 2001 and 2011 show increasing urban sprawl on the periphery, a trend which does not bode well for travelling times between home and work or school.

Labour market

South Africa's high unemployment is particularly severe amongst the black African population. There are vast differences between population groups in terms of unemployment, with little change in the pattern between them in recent years. On the expanded definition there were 8 million unemployed black Africans in 2016 (an unemployment rate of 41%). There were 0.6 million coloureds unemployed (28% unemployment rate), 0.1 million Indians/Asians (17%), and 0.2 million whites (9%). Unemployment is particularly severe amongst black African youth aged 15 to 34, with over 5 million unemployed in 2016 (53% unemployment rate) (Stats SA, 2018).

In 2016, 58% of the black African and 57% of the coloured labour forces had not achieved matric. Corresponding proportions for the Indian/Asian and white groups were 23% and 13%, respectively. Between 2008 and 2016, the proportion of the white labour force with a tertiary qualification increased from 42% to 45%, while the corresponding change in the black African labour force was from 9% to 12% (Stats SA, 2018).

For all age groups combined, i.e. 15–64 years, there were clear gains in skills between 1994 and 2016 in all population groups except black African. Coloureds increased from 11.6% to 20.6% (i.e. coloured skilled employment as a percentage of total coloured employment). Indians/Asians increased from 25.2% to 49.4% and whites increased from 42.2% to 61%. Black Africans increased marginally from 15.1% to 16.5% (Stats SA, 2018).

Amongst the youth, i.e. age groups 15–24 and 25–34, there were increases in skilled employment (as a proportion of corresponding total employment) between 1994 and 2016 in all population groups except black African. The black African proportions fell from 9.3% to 9% (15–24) and from 17.5% to 14.1% (25–34). Between 2013 and 2015, not only did the proportions decline, but the absolute numbers of young black Africans in skilled employment declined by 25,000 (15–24) and 55,000 (25–34). There were gains in 2016 in proportions and absolute numbers, but these were relatively small (Stats SA, 2018).

Even within the educated elite, namely graduates, the differences in unemployment rates are large among young people (ages 15–34). There is much higher unemployment amongst young black African graduates compared with the other population groups, with the gap getting worse over time. The trend raises concerns about the quality of qualifications and/or labour market discrimination.

Drivers of poverty

According to the Community Survey of 2016, unemployment as a driver of poverty was growing the fastest; jointly with poor educational attainment these accounted for about 60% of drivers of poverty. And amongst the youth, the main contributor to poverty is lack of educational attainment (Stats SA, 2016).

However, a ranking of perceptions (Stats SA, 2016) regarding the challenges that people face shows inadequate educational facilities as quite far down the list at number 15. This poses interesting questions for leaders at all levels of government. The Fees Must Fall campaign at South African universities, in the context of many other funding requests across the fiscal spectrum, asks the country to confront difficult choices about the allocation of financial resources. If an important dimension of sustainable development is quality education for all, but citizens' perceptions are inconsistent with that (because their attention is focused on more immediate needs like clean, accessible and affordable water), politicians and civil servants must work extra hard to achieve outcomes that will serve the long-term interests of communities while at the same time demonstrating their commitment to resolving the burning issues of the present. The preface to this report sets out the concept of the Overton window. Considering how complex society can be, particularly in a country of great diversity such as South Africa, there may be many Overton windows. For instance, the idea of 'quality education for all' alone is quite complex. It does not mean that everyone should receive the same education – not all of us can or wish to reach PhD status; if quality of education for all, or some variation thereof, is a policy goal, it must surely be pursued according to people's abilities and preferences. Leaders face the difficult question of where their Overton windows lie in the context of socio-economic challenges of addressing inequality, unemployment and poverty.

Conclusion

A demographic dividend is not a strategy for economic growth. Rather, it is the additional economic growth associated with a demographic transition, provided that the economy is already sufficiently strong to support low unemployment and that appropriate socio-economic conditions are in place, such as quality education for the growing number of working-age people to acquire the skills required by employers. Perhaps there were signs of a South African dividend during the high-growth years of 2005 to 2007, but those are a distant memory.

South Africa's national development plan (NDP) carries the title *Our future – make it work*. It has a vision (many visions) for 2030. Time is short. Policy makers, past and present, have done much for socio-economic transformation, but today's leaders carry the responsibility to achieve so much more. One lesson that the demographic dividend literature teaches is that opportunities come and go. Opportunities, or what is left of them, need to be embraced to the full.

South Africa's demographic opportunity is the transition from a working-age ratio of 57% in 1985 to 65% today. It may not go any higher. The demographic transition has not provided a demographic dividend nationally, and if anything can be done to salvage a portion of the country's potential dividend for the future, it must be implemented now and with the utmost urgency. Since 1994, worthy social and economic plans have come and gone, and to the extent that they have successfully driven socio-economic transformation within a responsible fiscal framework, they deserve credit in spades. But they have not been enough, at least not in terms of vigorous implementation, to put South Africa onto the high-growth path it desperately needs and which is a fundamental requirement for the further growth that can emanate from demographics. By 2030, today's primary school children will be old enough to ask hard questions regarding what more could and should have been done. If we continue to fall short, what will we tell them?

There is abundant policy advice for South Africa from the IMF and OECD and other international organisations regarding the path to sustainable economic growth and development. Neither is there a shortage of advice at home, be it from labour, business, civil society or government itself, the NDP being a prominent case in point. A comprehensive assessment of all the policy options is beyond the scope of this paper, but many South Africans would agree with the following aspirations:

- using technology and all other means available to educate the current and future generations of young people, such that they have the skills to participate fully in the economy of the future (we cannot know precisely what that future will look like and precisely what skills will be needed, but strong foundations can nevertheless be put in place by pushing mathematics and science.);
- smoothing the way for small business to flourish (less red tape, more support for entrepreneurs);
- co-operation between the public and private sectors to make broadband services widely available at internationally competitive costs;
- for goods and services built on new and 'disruptive' technology, maintaining law and order and promoting level-playing fields and co-operation between old and new;
- resolving the policy uncertainty and acrimony in the mining industry;
- finding cost-effective solutions to the many disparities in healthcare;
- managerial excellence at the state-owned enterprises, such that they provide cost-effective services across the spectrum (from low-income households to big business), without consuming endless amounts of taxpayers' resources;
- managerial excellence across government departments and agencies at all levels (national, provincial and municipal);
- clean governance, in particular a thorough crackdown on corruption from top to bottom in both the public and private sectors; and

- effective investigation and prosecution of all forms of crime.

Other countries in Africa are still going through a demographic transition and their potential dividend lies ahead. Whether or not South Africa's demographic transition can still be translated into a partial dividend, let the African continent learn this from the South African experience: do all that is possible and as soon as possible to put in place supporting socio-economic conditions. Dividends are not free gifts, they must be earned; their availability is not there forever, but subject to a window of opportunity. Let us make sure that one day we do not lament their passing, but rather celebrate their success. The Overton window of political possibilities can be a useful interlocutor for advancing radical as well as nascent and well-founded social concerns such as the question of whether South Africa or indeed Africa is poised for a demographic dividend. Milton Friedman commenting on capitalism is said to have articulated the Overton window of political possibilities with the phrase 'until the politically impossible becomes the politically inevitable'. The demographic dividend question is in this category of the urgent and critical for Africa and South Africa.

References

Ahmed, S.A., M. Cruz, B. Quillin & P. Schellekens, P. 2016. Demographic change and development: Looking at challenges and opportunities through a new typology', Policy Research Working Paper 7893, Development Prospects Group, Development Economics, World Bank.

Bloom, D.E., D. Canning & J. Sevilla. 2003. *The Demographic Dividend: A New Perspective on the Economic Consequences of Population Change.* RAND: Santa Monica. Available at: https://www.rand.org/content/dam/rand/pubs/monograph_reports/2007/MR1274.pdf [Accessed on 17 October 2018].

Canning, D., S. Raja & A.S. Yazbeck, eds. 2015. *Africa's Demographic Transition: Dividend or Disaster?* Africa Development Forum series. Washington, DC: World Bank. doi:10.1596/978-1-4648-0489-2. License: Creative Commons Attribution CC BY 3.0 IGO.

Drummond, P., V. Thakoor & S. Yu. 2014. 'Africa rising: Harnessing the demographic dividend', IMF Working Paper WP/14/143, International Monetary Fund.

IMF (International Monetary Fund). 2016. 'South Africa. Country Report No. 16/217'. Available at: https://www.imf.org/external/pubs/ft/scr/2016/cr16217.pdf [Accessed on 15 October 2018].

IMF (International Monetary Fund). 2017. South Africa. Country Report No. 17/189. Available at: http://www.treasury.gov.za/publications/other/imf/2017/IMF%20Art%20IV%20report.pdf [Accessed on 15 October 2018].

Lehohla, P. 2017. 'Wither a demographic dividend South Africa: The "Overton Window" of political possibilities'. Available at: http://www.statssa.gov.za/publications/OP001/OP0012017.pdf [Accessed on 15 October 2018].

National Treasury (South Africa). 2017. 'Budget review 2017'. Available at: http://www.treasury.gov.za/documents/national%20budget/2017/review/FullBR.pdf [Accessed on 17 October 2018].

NPC (National Planning Commission) (South Africa). 2012. *National Development Plan 2030: Our Future – Make It Work*. Available at: http://www.dac.gov.za/sites/default/files/NDP%202030%20-%20Our%20future%20-%20make%20it%20work_0.pdf [Accessed on 15 October 2018].

OECD (Organisation for Economic Co-operation and Development). 2017. *OECD Economic Surveys: South Africa 2017*. OECD Publishing, Paris. Available at: http://dx.doi.org/10.1787/eco_surveys-zaf-2017-en [Accessed 25 October 2018].

SARB (South African Reserve Bank). 2017. 'Selected forecast results: MPC meeting', September 2017.

Stats SA. 2016. 'Community Survey 2016'. Available at: http://cs2016.statssa.gov.za/wp-content/uploads/2016/07/NT-30-06-2016-RELEASE-for-CS-2016-_Statistical-releas_1-July-2016.pdf [Accessed on 17 October 2018].

Stats SA. 2018. 'QLFS Trends 2008–2018 Q2'. Available at: http://www.statssa.gov.za/?page_id=1854&PPN=P0211 [Accessed on 15 October 2018].

World Bank. 1993. *The East Asian Miracle*. Oxford: Oxford University Press.

WORLDS APART: SPATIAL INEQUALITIES IN SOUTH AFRICA

Ivan Turok

'The spatial legacy of apartheid separates the majority of people from economic activity, traps disadvantaged communities in poverty and underdevelopment, creates inefficient cities and robs poor, rural people of secure livelihoods.' – Motlanthe High Level Panel, 2017: 36–7

Introduction

THE SPATIAL ORGANISATION OF THE ECONOMY and society really matters. Dense, well-connected settlements can improve prosperity and social cohesion, while dispersed settlements tend to exclude people from opportunities and reinforce social divisions. The geography of inequality in South Africa has been neglected over the last two decades, despite the centrality of racial segregation to colonialism and apartheid. The government's equivocal and indecisive approach to spatial divides means that the scars of history remain largely intact. Indeed, the tendency to neglect the spatial dimension of poverty and inequality means that people's own efforts to erode the geography of apartheid are unrecognised and disregarded. This contradicts the spirit of the Constitution and hinders economic and social transformation.

A recent report confirms that South Africa is probably the most unequal and unevenly developed country in the world (World Bank, 2018). This is unhealthy, unfair and destabilising. Spatial gaps in material and subjective well-being are stark and deeply etched into the landscape. Within every city and town, exclusive business precincts and upmarket suburbs with first-rate amenities are juxtaposed with overcrowded townships and squalid shack settlements. In rural areas, remote villages with mud schools and no piped water contrast with luxurious game lodges and affluent country estates. Such conspicuous spatial divides create perceptions of injustice and resentment (Motlanthe High Level Panel, 2017). Growing up in different worlds with incomparable social infrastructure and opportunities of all kinds shapes life chances profoundly and corrodes trust across society. Many poor communities feel left behind with no stake in the country's success. Entrenched geographical inequalities also create inefficiencies and dampen aggregate growth. They cause wasteful use of land, impose costs on the movement of people and goods between areas, and raise barriers to business interaction and trade.

The existence of extreme spatial disparities is partly a legacy of racial separation imposed under colonialism and apartheid through vicious regimes of land dispossession, forced removals, influx controls, residential segregation, vastly unequal education systems and so on. Other factors are responsible for the persistence of these patterns, including concentrated economic power, inertia in the built environment and continuing unevenness in institutional capabilities across the country (Todes & Turok, 2017). Geographical divisions persist despite important constitutional rights, a welter of legislation, common institutional structures, sizeable fiscal transfers from leading to lagging regions, and many programmes and projects intended to promote social justice, rural development and land restitution. Spatial inequalities clearly have multiple dimensions, which are difficult to overcome. Undoing the damage of apartheid to normalise spatial forms will require greater vision, co-ordination and sustained commitment across government. There are trade-offs involved that necessitate decision makers making more deliberate choices.

Since 1994, issues of space, place and territory have not received the attention they deserve. For example, the government has been ambivalent about internal shifts in the population, despite increasing evidence that this can help to lift people out of poverty and promote income mobility (CDE, 2017; Schotte et al, 2017; Visagie & Turok, forthcoming). Housing policies have failed to accommodate most migrant households and have compounded hardship and exclusion by dispersing poor communities to the outskirts of cities, far from economic opportunities, good schools, training colleges and other facilities. More explicit initiatives to reduce spatial disparities have been fragmentary and short-lived rather than integrated and sustained (Todes & Turok, 2017).

Spatial inequalities in South Africa are usually conceived of as a simple urban-rural divide (World Bank, 2018). This is limiting because it ignores the relationships between urban and rural areas and it obscures the enormous differences across both urban and rural localities. The challenges facing commercial farming areas differ greatly from the former homelands, and big cities have little in common with small towns. Given South Africa's large and expansive territory, spatial patterns should be understood and tackled at two distinct scales – regions and sub-regions (focusing on cities).

The purpose of this short chapter is to consider the nature and dynamics of spatial inequalities in South Africa in order to identify potential responses that could support more inclusive forms of development. I analyse some of the prevailing patterns and driving forces that lie behind them. This is necessarily selective and pitched at a high level of generality.

The physical separation between people and productive activity

The twin pillars of spatial development are the distribution of jobs and population. Colonial and apartheid governments tended to force (black) people apart from economic opportunities, at great cost to individuals, families and communities. More than two decades after apartheid, there continues to be a gulf between where many people live and where jobs and resources are concentrated. This aggravates unemployment and poverty for people living in the periphery, and imposes additional costs on their mobility. The exceptional transport expenditures are like a residual burden on the poor lingering long after apartheid. The physical disconnection, or 'spatial mismatch' (Budlender & Royston, 2016), applies at both the regional scale (between cities and isolated rural areas) and at the metropolitan scale (between the core centres of employment and the main townships).

Contemporary forces of economic agglomeration tend to reproduce this pattern, as prosperity reinforces business confidence in better-off areas, and the creation of wealth and income generates further resources that get reinvested locally – in other businesses, up-market property, consumer services, private schools, hospitals and all kinds of amenities. In the absence of countervailing policies, such as a requirement on private developers to provide mixed-income/ inclusionary housing, low-income groups and small enterprises can easily get squeezed out of productive places through the operation of the land and housing market. This cumulative process of uneven development has far-reaching implications for living standards and human progress in different places. Uneven economic performance also influences the revenues available to municipalities and their capacity to deliver decent and dependable services to local citizens and firms.

Despite the existence of many national policies, a unitary system of provincial and local government and universal social protections, sharp spatial divides persist. Relatively affluent localities have superior economic infrastructure, better education and healthcare facilities, more reliable electricity and sanitation networks, more attractive public spaces and a wider range of recreational facilities. These 'positive externalities' improve people's living conditions and enhance their chances of success in life. Conversely, poorer localities tend to offer fewer livelihood opportunities, inferior public infrastructure and more mediocre services. These communities experience greater insecurity, worse social problems, greater health hazards, higher risks of disaster, and much more crime and violence. Growing up in harsh and inhospitable environments makes it far more difficult for people to realise their potential. Their restricted prospects for social advancement also hamper their contribution to the economy as workers and consumers.

There are dangers in South Africa's uniform policy and regulatory framework that people with low incomes are forced to live in places where it is cheap and easy to build, rather than in places with stronger economies and more jobs. Within cities, this is because housing subsidies are skewed towards low-cost land and poor households can only afford marginal sites. Land-use regulations and environmental controls are also more relaxed further away from affluent suburbs and business precincts, where NIMBY (not in my backyard) attitudes obstruct low-income developments. Outside the cities this is because poorer municipalities are more desperate for development, needs-driven government funding pushes housing and social infrastructure towards lagging areas, and housing is one of the few tangibles that politicians can deliver to hard-pressed communities experiencing de-industrialisation and mining closures. But does it make sense to invest scarce public resources to build houses in isolated locations with uncertain economic futures, especially when many people's aspirations seem to lie in the towns and cities where they stand a better chance of getting a job? The Constitution enabled the state to intervene in the urban land market to reverse the effects of apartheid, but the political will to use existing legal powers has been lacking (Turok, 2016). The state has not even used its own surplus land holdings to boost house building in well-located areas. A recent surge in urban land occupations and invasions suggests that people's tolerance of apartheid's cruel geography is diminishing (*Business Day*, 2018).

Broad spatial patterns

One of the most striking features of South Africa's spatial economy is the concentration of activity in Gauteng. The province generates more than a third of the country's economic output, despite having only 2% of the land area and just under a quarter of the population. Gauteng has the highest GDP per capita and average income of all the provinces (Turok et al, 2017). Relatively high productivity helps to explain why its jobs growth has outpaced other provinces since the 1990s. This reflects the region's economic scale and density, which reduces transport costs, promotes business efficiency and specialisation, and improves face-to-face communication, knowledge spill-overs and localised learning. Relatively strong employment growth helps to explain why the rate of unemployment and poverty are lower than elsewhere (World Bank, 2018). Concentrated opportunities have made the region a magnet for in-migration from the rest of the country and other parts of southern Africa (CDE, 2017). In short, there is an economic and social dynamism in Gauteng that is not apparent elsewhere. The main employment centres are in the metros of Johannesburg, Tshwane (Pretoria) and Ekurhuleni (East Rand).

Other concentrations of economic activity are in the Western Cape (centred on Cape Town) and KwaZulu-Natal (centred on eThekwini (Durban)). Secondary cities include Nelson Mandela Bay (Port Elizabeth), Buffalo City (East London), Mangaung (Bloemfontein) and Msunduzi (Pietermaritzburg). The economic performance of all these cities has lagged behind Gauteng, although they have outpaced the rest of the country.

Outside the cities, the population is unevenly distributed across the countryside. The distinction between the former homelands and commercial farming areas is vital. Under apartheid the original population of the homelands was inflated by forced removals from the cities and towns, and by restrictions on out-migration. In contrast, the commercial farming areas experienced de-population following the mechanisation of agriculture and farm evictions. These historic differences remain important sources of social and economic contrast today, although there are some signs that the gaps are receding as people move from impoverished areas and resettle closer to economic centres.

Uneven growth

Two-thirds of economic output in SA is produced by just three provinces – Gauteng, KwaZulu-Natal and the Western Cape (Turok et al, 2017). They have more diversified economies than the rest of the country. Another three provinces account for only about 10% of aggregate output – the Northern Cape, Free State and North West. Their economies are relatively dependent on mining and agriculture. In between, the economies of the Eastern Cape, Mpumalanga and Limpopo are roughly similar in size to each other.

The relative importance of the three largest provinces to national GDP has increased over the last two decades, so South Africa's economy has become more concentrated over time. Gauteng's share has risen from 32% in 1994 to 34.7% in 2014. The smallest provincial economies have contracted in relative terms. The provincial pecking order has not changed over this period, suggesting considerable path dependency in their trajectories. This reflects the general lack of dynamism and diversification within the economy. It also hints at the difficulties involved in developing new industrial paths to transform established economic structures. The challenges of structural reform include spreading prosperity beyond the core regions to places that consistently lag behind.

The relative growth of the metropolitan regions compared with more rural regions suggests that the forces of agglomeration consistently outweigh those of deconcentration and dispersal. This city-centred dynamic has been apparent throughout the world in recent decades (Brulhart & Sbergami, 2009; Polese, 2009; United Nations, 2016; Lall et al, 2017). There have been many explanations offered (see Table 8.1), the relative importance of which has not been established in South Africa.

A significant motivation for businesses clustering together is that this enables proximity to specialised suppliers and shared services. Being embedded in business networks helps firms to cope with intensified competition by focusing on their core competences and outsourcing other tasks to local suppliers. Another explanation reflects the increasing value of knowledge and innovation for business competitiveness. This demands good access to human capital, advanced technology and universities. A third explanation relates to the superior physical and communications infrastructure available in big cities, including airports and broadband. A fourth reflects household aspirations for better living standards and superior social, educational and recreational amenities, which drives consumption demand. The threat of climate change and water scarcity in agricultural regions may be another driver of economic concentration.

Table 8.1: Forces for spatial concentration and dispersal

Forces for spatial concentration	Forces for dispersal
Business clustering and networks	Cost-saving for routine manufacturing
Access to knowledge and innovation	Exploitation of new mineral resources
Proximity to advanced skill-sets	Revival of agricultural production
International connectivity infrastructure	Growth of nature-based tourism
Consumer aspirations	Expansion of renewable energy
Climate change	

Of course, economic pressures also work in the opposite direction. Dispersal may be promoted by routine manufacturing industries seeking lower property and labour costs and less congestion outside the big cities. The extraction of new mineral resources and the revival of agriculture may also encourage deconcentration. The growth of nature-based tourism and renewable energy in the form of wind and solar power also tend to support the dispersal of activity to the countryside. The relative importance of these forces can change over time, depending on the technologies and cost drivers. Looking to the future, the role of knowledge, digital technology and advanced skills are bound to increase, all of which tend to encourage concentration. It is very costly for the state to steer business location decisions in a contrary direction.

Spatial redistribution

Persistent inequalities do not mean that the provincial economies exist in isolation of each other or that they have been left to their own devices. There are several ways in which the benefits of growing cities (the urban 'dividend') have been shared with lagging regions. One of the main ways is through fiscal transfers by the state. The government takes a share of the taxes paid in the most productive regions and redistributes it to poorer areas. It does so for reasons of national cohesion and social justice, and as an expression of solidarity between better-off and poorer communities. Large-scale fiscal redistribution is a major departure from the past, when privileged areas retained the bulk of their tax revenues. Most of the redistributed funding is spent on social programmes, including education, healthcare, social grants, housing subsidies and basic services. Poorer regions benefit disproportionately because they have higher social needs and infrastructure backlogs. Current national debates about inclusive growth and radical transformation overlook the sizeable spatial transfers that occur behind the scenes without any fanfare.

The most important source of taxation in South Africa is personal income tax (PIT). The share of national PIT paid by the three provinces of Gauteng, Western Cape and KwaZulu-Natal is 75%. The other six provinces pay only a quarter of the total. Gauteng alone pays 46.2% – nearly as much as all the other provinces combined (National Treasury, 2017). This is partly because there is more economic activity in Gauteng than elsewhere, hence there are more jobs and taxpayers. It is also because Gauteng's economy is more productive in terms of its industries and occupations. There are more high-level occupations and advanced functions, and more highly skilled jobs that pay higher salaries and more taxes. Nearly a third (29%) of Gauteng's jobs are professional, technical or managerial, compared with only one-seventh (14%) in the Northern Cape.

In addition to the bigger total contribution to national taxes, each Gauteng resident pays more than twice as much PIT as people in every other province. This indicates that average earnings and employment levels in Gauteng are higher than elsewhere. Lower taxes paid in other provinces reflect lower salaries, less-skilled occupations and higher unemployment rates. Gauteng is clearly the golden goose of the South African economy.

The extent of fiscal redistribution between the provinces and municipalities is shown in Figure 8.1. This reveals the average financial

Figure 8.1: Fiscal allocations to provinces and municipalities

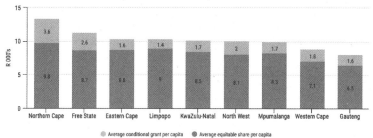

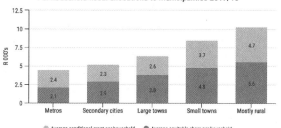

Source: National Treasury, 2017

allocation per person for each province and the allocation per household for different categories of municipality. The Northern Cape receives much more funding per person than anywhere else. The poorest rural provinces of Eastern Cape and Limpopo receive about a quarter more than Gauteng. The government is clearly reallocating resources on a large scale, bearing in mind that Gauteng residents pay more taxes than the other provinces and its population is growing more rapidly.

There is even more redistribution between municipalities. The Treasury allocates more than double the funding per household to rural municipalities than it does to the metros. This is partly because the metros have an economic base that enables them to raise their own property taxes. The level of redistribution between the municipalities can be summarised in the following way. The eight metros generate 70% of PIT and receive 31% of local government transfers, while the 61 rural municipalities also receive 31% of transfers, but pay only 5% of PIT (National Treasury, 2017). The extent of reallocation should be seen as a major achievement in enabling essential services to be extended to under-served communities. However, there are bound to be questions about whether this should continue at the same level in conditions of low growth when the metros are under acute strain from expanding populations and infrastructure bottlenecks. There are also questions about whether rural spending could be reoriented to achieve a bigger developmental impact beyond service delivery by doing more to improve local skills, diversify local economies and strengthen livelihoods to raise household incomes and promote dignity and self-determination.

Rural-urban migration

People are not passive spectators of spatial inequalities. They have agency and many of them make deliberate choices to migrate in the face of better economic opportunities elsewhere. This can help to reduce the level of unemployment in the countryside. Apartheid imposed strict controls on migration, although it remained a vital mechanism for men to seek work in the mines and urban centres, and to remit resources to families left behind. Migration accelerated when influx controls were removed in the 1980s, and South Africa's internal settlement structure began to shift towards a more conventional pattern. In recent years the rate of domestic migration appears to have moderated (Turok, 2014). This is probably linked to the economic slowdown and the shortfall of job opportunities in the cities.

Despite the stalled economy, recent research using a unique

source of longitudinal data reveals that migration helps people to get out of poverty. As a result, migrants tend to be better off than people who remain in the countryside. Estimates from the National Income Dynamics Study indicate that as many as 385,000 people were lifted above the poverty line between 2008 and 2014 in the course of moving from rural to urban areas (Visagie & Turok, forthcoming). They became better off by clambering onto the labour market or into informal work. At the outset in 2008, over 80% of migrants were destitute in their rural communities.[20] Six years later, only 35% of them were still below the poverty line. Meanwhile, 70% of the rural residents who chose not to migrate remained poor. The improvement in incomes for migrants was matched by a reduction in unemployment, which fell from 50% in 2008 to 15% in 2014. An estimated 330,000 people moved into employment after migrating to an urban area. Half of them were previously unemployed and half were not economically active.

A major hurdle facing migrants is the lack of affordable housing in the cities, which forces people onto unsuitable land or into substandard accommodation, typically an unauthorised shack or sometimes a 'bad building'. Many of them are vulnerable to displacement, harassment or eviction by private property owners or an arm of the state. Ethnic and regional differences may also be exploited to reinforce their precarious position. The indignity and insecurity of informal shelter tends to produce a circular form of migration, whereby people retain a base in their rural area. They return to this home periodically, when they can afford to do so, and do not commit fully to living in the city. They lead a kind of dual existence, which is far less satisfactory than having a single place of belonging where they could invest in a single housing unit, build up an asset and experience a more rounded and rewarding lifestyle.

---

20   Migrants are defined as adults (aged 19–56) who were rural in the first wave and moved to an urban area subsequently, and did not move back to a rural area.

The strength and direction of migration flows illustrate the contrasting economic fortunes of the provinces. Gauteng has consistently been the biggest recipient of net migration flows, with over 1.5 million individuals between 2001 and 2016. The Western Cape came next with 450,000 net migrants. KwaZulu-Natal has experienced equivalent numbers of in- and out-migrants, reflecting its weaker economy than the other two. The biggest sources of net out-migration have been the Eastern Cape and Limpopo, reflecting the presence of the former homelands within these provinces.

The employment rate (the proportion of adults with a job) provides a measure of the relative strength of regional economies. The employment rate is over 52% in the Gauteng metros, despite high in-migration, but only 20.8% in the former homelands. Lack of employment is a potent 'push' factor encouraging out-migration. The employment rate is 45% in the coastal metros, 43% in the secondary cities and 41% in the commercial farming areas. The high employment rate in Gauteng indicates relatively strong demand for labour, reflecting the more robust economy.

The scale of internal migration has been substantial, but insufficient as yet to eliminate the gap between the geography of population and jobs. Over 14 million people (more than a quarter of South African citizens) continue to live in the former homelands, despite their weak economies. The total population of these areas has been stable over the last 15 years, because natural growth has compensated for the numbers of people moving out. The population of the Gauteng metros has increased by nearly four million (49%) over the same period. South Africa's shifting population over the last two decades has broadly followed the pattern of employment growth. This is a much healthier situation than the extreme mismatch that prevailed under apartheid. The normalisation of South Africa's geography is socially disruptive, but essential for sustainable economic growth, equality of opportunity and cultural dynamism (Makgetla, 2018).

New marginalised places

Poor communities have responded to the shortage of affordable accommodation and the slow pace of house-building in the cities in various ways, including land occupations, invasions of derelict inner city buildings, and erecting dwellings (usually shacks) in other people's backyards. The most important numerically has been the growth of backyarding. Between 2001 and 2011, the number of households living in backyard shacks increased by 55% (from 460,000 to 713,000), while the number living in free-standing shacks actually decreased by 126,900 to 1,249,800 (Turok & Borel-Saladin, 2016). Some backyards have been in older urban neighbourhoods, such as Yeoville and Bertrams in Johannesburg. The scale has been much larger in established townships, including Soweto, Tembisa and Tokoza. There have also been numerous backyard developments in newer RDP settlements, such as Diepsloot and Cosmo City in Johannesburg, and Du Noon and Joe Slovo Park in Cape Town. This is a novel feature of the post-apartheid period. It remains poorly researched and inadequately understood. This is mirrored by a curious vacuum in national housing policy because backyard dwellings are regarded as non-compliant with building and planning codes, and therefore illegal.

Yet there are several positive features of the backyard phenomenon, which suggest that it should be taken more seriously as part of urban housing policy. First, backyard dwellings enlarge the housing stock and provide much-needed flexible rental accommodation at no cost to the public purse. Second, backyard structures are often better located in relation to job opportunities than dormitory townships. They may offer families better access to basic services within the yard and higher levels of personal safety than living in an informal settlement. Third, backyard dwellings provide a regular source of income to homeowners, most of whom are poor and unemployed. The rent is sometimes their only source of income, so it is a vital source of social protection. There are also signs of enterprising owners emerging who use the income stream to finance more substantial improvements to the backyard structures, including constructing additional and higher quality units. This increases the supply of decent and yet still affordable rental housing in the city.

These attributes need to be set against certain drawbacks of backyard development. First, the townships were not planned for the level of population densities currently being experienced. Consequently, the infrastructure and services are often overloaded, resulting in blocked pipes and service breakdowns. Second, the high residential densities and pressure on public services can exacerbate the risks of pollution, contagious diseases, electrocution and social conflict. Overloaded electricity networks are notoriously fragile and susceptible to failure. Domestic fires spread rapidly when shacks are built cheek by jowl and across property boundaries. Third, informal backyard structures are often constructed without any technical input or compliance with building standards. Shacks built of rudimentary material lower the tone of the neighbourhood and do not provide effective protection from the elements. Two- or three-storey makeshift structures periodically collapse, and the lack of formal approvals limits the long-term value of the assets. Fourth, tenants lack any tenure security and are vulnerable to exploitation by unscrupulous landlords.

Immense social and financial pressures are accumulating in some of these intensively built-up areas. Communities are suspicious of all government entities because of the neglect, and social trust is lacking. There is often little respect for the law, electricity theft is high, encroachment on streets, pavements and other public spaces is widespread, and protests are common. Social stresses and resentment about having to pay rent regularly spills over into invasions of nearby land parcels. Municipalities struggle to cope with maintaining the infrastructure and delivering essential services, and they lack the skill-sets required to understand and engage effectively with disenchanted local communities. These marginalised places are distinctive to the post-apartheid era, and the situation is often complicated by the arrival of foreign nationals. These are proving to be extremely difficult to manage, so they often get ignored. This is very risky because tensions could boil over and the situation could erupt. This has happened recently in Johannesburg's Rosettenville and in Cape Town's Du Noon. An energetic, hands-on approach to urban land is required to release surplus public property for serviced sites, low-income housing and related facilities. A new commitment to work in partnership with communities is also vital to build trust and harness the energy of civil society for more constructive purposes.

Poverty and deprivation on the periphery

Aliber et al (2016) suggest that livelihood opportunities have improved in the former homelands in recent years through higher consumer spending following the expansion of social grants and government jobs. The reliance on fiscal transfers from elsewhere means that this consumption-based activity is susceptible to shifts in public policy and the state of the fiscus. One symptom is the growth of the minibus taxi industry, which has both created jobs and improved connectivity with the cities. Construction activity has expanded as a result of state infrastructure spending and individual house-building. It has created backward and forward linkages to the local economy, including suppling building materials. Meanwhile, the agriculture sector has not performed well, despite positive government intentions. Evidence that scattered rural communities are consolidating around denser economic nodes and along transport corridors is important in suggesting that more viable settlements are emerging. This resettlement process should be actively supported because these places are more cost-effective to service and could generate greater economies of scale in consumption and production.

Labour market conditions are better in the metros, where a much higher proportion of adults are in employment and adding to family incomes. There is little sign of any narrowing of the gap in economic circumstances between the different settlement types over the last two decades (World Bank, 2018). The economic gulf between different parts of the country is matched by big inequalities in access to basic public services, including water, sanitation, electricity and refuse collection (Stats SA, 2017). As a result of targeted state investment, these gaps have narrowed since the 1990s in some respects – particularly electricity – but less so in other respects – particularly sanitation and refuse removal. Improvements in the former homelands have lagged behind other areas (Turok et al, 2017). Weak institutional capacity and mismanagement seem to be serious problems. The appalling state of affairs in some places was revealed by the recent furore over a young girl drowning after falling into an unsafe pit latrine at her school in Bizana in the Eastern Cape (Dyantyi, 2018). A similar tragic incident occurred in Limpopo when a young boy fell into a collapsed pit latrine at school in 2014.

Conclusion: Towards a more effective state response

The government's response to spatial inequalities has not been consistent. As we have seen, substantial tax revenues have been skewed towards rural communities through social grants and spending on municipal services, health and education. This has tended to compensate poorer locations for their weak economies rather than to create the conditions for productive investment and self-sustaining growth. More deliberate, spatially targeted efforts to stimulate economic development have been piecemeal and poorly aligned (Todes & Turok, 2017). The impact of many separate initiatives across government has been diluted by the absence of any overarching spatial policy to integrate them. The lack of a national territorial plan or framework is surprising considering the enduring spatial divides inherited from apartheid. The government's ambivalent stance towards internal resettlement processes is also curious and perhaps even unconstitutional in undermining national citizenship and the freedom of movement. Many of the people living in informal settlements in cities and mining towns are still treated as temporary migrants, instead of permanent citizens with rights to public services.

Turning to the future, an important area for government improvement is to react more quickly and resolutely to population shifts in order to alleviate the multiple pressures and problems that result. State resources and institutional support need to respond more swiftly to burgeoning needs so as to avoid situations like Marikana, where Rustenberg municipality simply couldn't cope with a 75% increase in its population between 1996 and 2011 as a result of the platinum boom. The metros are even larger pressure cookers, evident in escalating social protests and land invasions. State institutions need more timely information and intelligence than they currently have available to deal promptly with a fluid population that is reshaping society, culture and politics in a very dynamic fashion. Internal migration is also slowly and ineluctably eroding the geography of apartheid.

Looking ahead, population mobility and settlement patterns are bound to transform further as a result of climate change, food insecurity and water scarcity. An economic recovery will also spur domestic and international migration flows, especially if – as seems likely – jobs are created more quickly in the big cities. The metros need additional resources, technical capacity and streamlined procedures to cope with the rising demand for basic services, schools, healthcare and so on. The whole apparatus and regulatory systems of government are sluggish about the provision of essential facilities in response to population movements, causing immense frustration and suffering among families forced to endure overcrowded, insanitary and hazardous living conditions for year after year.

It is even more important for the government to plan ahead for future settlement growth. It is far more cost-effective to prepare for urban development in advance of land being occupied, than to try and correct a disorderly situation after the fact. Planning ahead includes acquiring and allocating land for housing and related uses, and installing basic infrastructure and public-transport systems. Trying to upgrade or retrofit informal settlements that are poorly laid out once they have already been occupied is inevitably contentious and costly because people resist disruption and relocation. The government needs to be more strategic in allocating resources and not simply follow past trends in a passive manner. It needs to embark on the difficult task of formulating a spatial vision and framework to encourage development into suitable locations for human settlement, taking into account economic realities as well as pressing social needs and no-go areas for the natural environment. Greater coordination across silos and deliberate engagement with the private sector are also essential for this to be effective. There is no reason why the government should not require all new developments to include a share of low-income housing.

Summing up, the government needs a single spatial plan that cuts across its silos to guide public investment and to manage social expectations and environmental risks. This plan needs to recognise the linkages and interdependence between places and not treat them in isolation. Urban and rural areas need to be planned within their city-regional context, recognising the intense flows of people and resources across administrative boundaries. A national spatial framework should recognise the distinctive role of secondary cities and towns that serve as regional service centres. Some of them may be able to help absorb some of the pressures currently facing the big metros. Individual cities also interact strongly with each other as part of a national urban system that needs to be better understood. Indeed, the metros are embedded in a bigger international network of cities that offers both opportunities and constraints for accelerated economic development. A fuller appreciation of how South Africa functions as a place would assist in formulating more effective responses. Supplementing the traditional systems of land-use regulation and development restraint with a more proactive approach to managing urban land is also urgent.

Considerable thanks to Justin Visagie for assistance with the data analysis. The chapter draws on a report prepared for the Motlanthe High Level Parliamentary Panel (Turok et al, 2017).

References
Aliber, M., M. Maswana, N. Nikelo, B. Mbantsa & L. Bank. 2016. 'Economic development in South Africa's former homelands and rural-urban linkages', REDI 3x3 paper.

Brulhart, M. & F. Sbergami. 2009. 'Agglomeration and growth: Cross-country evidence'. *Journal of Urban Economics*, 65(1): 48–63.

Budlender, J. & L. Royston. 2016. 'Edged out: Spatial mismatch and spatial justice in South Africa's main urban centre', Socio Economic Rights Institute. Johannesburg, South Africa.

Business Day. 2018. 'Sound housing policy needed'. Editorial, 28 March. Centre for Development and Enterprise. 2017. *Opportunities First.* Johannesburg: CDE.

Dyantyi, H. 2018. 'The indignity of pit toilet deaths', *Daily Maverick*, 16 March. Available at: www.dailymaverick.co.za [Accessed on 15 October 2018].

Lall, S., V. Henderson & T. Venables. 2017. *Africa's Cities: Opening Doors to the World.* Washington: World Bank.

Makgetla, N. 2018. 'SA must cater for new settlement patterns around cities'. *Business Day*, 13 March.

Motlanthe High Level Panel. 2017. 'Report on the assessment of key legislation and the acceleration of fundamental change, Executive Summary'. Available at: https://www.parliament.gov.za/high-level-panel [Accessed on 15 October 2018].

National Treasury. 2017. *Budget Review*. Available at: http://www.treasury. gov.za/documents/national%20budget/2017/review/FullBR.pdf [Accessed on 15 October 2018].

Polese, M. 2009. *The Wealth and Poverty of Regions: Why Cities Matter.* Chicago: The University of Chicago Press.

Schotte, S., R. Zizzamia & M. Leibbrandt. 2017. 'Social stratification, life chances and vulnerability to poverty in South Africa', SALDRU Working Paper 208, University of Cape Town.

Statistics South Africa. 2017. 'Poverty trends in South Africa: An examination of absolute poverty between 2006 and 2015.' Available at: https://www. statssa.gov.za/publications/Report-03-10-06/Report-03-10-062015.pdf [Accessed on 15 October 2018].

Todes, A. & I. Turok. 2017. 'Spatial inequalities and policies in South Africa: Place-based or people-centred?', *Progress in Planning.* Available at: http://dx.doi.org/10.1016/j.progress.2017.03.001 [Accessed on 15 October 2018].

Turok, I. 2014. 'South Africa's tortured urbanisation and the complications of reconstruction' , in G. Martine & G. McGranahan, eds. *Urban Growth in Emerging Economies: Lessons from the BRICS.* London: Routledge, pp 143–91.

Turok, I. 2016. 'South Africa's new urban agenda: Transformation of compensation?'. *Local Economy,* 31(1): 9–27.

Turok, I. & J. Borel-Saladin. 2016. 'Backyard shacks, informality and the urban housing crisis in South Africa: Stopgap or prototype solution?'. *Housing Studies,* 31(4): 384–409.

Turok, I., A. Scheba & J. Visagie. 2017. 'Reducing spatial inequalities through better regulation', Diagnostic report to the High Level Panel on the assessment of key legislation and the acceleration of fundamental change. Available at: https://www.parliament.gov.za/high-level-panel [Accessed on 15 October 2018].

United Nations. 2016. 'New Urban Agenda', Resolution 71/256, Adopted by the General Assembly on 23 December, New York.

Visagie, J. & I. Turok. (forthcoming). 'Rural-urban migration as a means of getting ahead', in L. Bank, ed. *Migrant Labour After Apartheid*. Pretoria: HSRC Press.

World Bank. 2018. *Overcoming Poverty and Inequality in South Africa.* Washington: World Bank. Available at: http://documents.worldbank. org/curated/en/530481521735906534/pdf/124521-REV-OUO-South-Africa-Poverty-and-Inequality-Assessment-Report-2018-FINAL-WEB.pdf [Accessed on 12 September 2018].

TACKLING PERSISTENT POVERTY
AND INEQUALITY:
A DYNAMIC PERSPECTIVE

Murray Leibbrandt, Simone Schotte and Rocco Zizzamia

POVERTY, INEQUALITY AND UNEMPLOYMENT in South Africa sustain each other in a symbiotic fashion. This negative symbiosis has thwarted policy efforts at dealing with any one of these phenomena in isolation, illustrating the difficulty, but also the necessity, of a coordinated effort to address all three. In this chapter, we add a dynamic perspective to the preceding chapters in order to shed light on the unequal economic and social conditions that create, exacerbate and perpetuate poverty and inequality over time.

Using data from the National Income Dynamics Study (NIDS), South Africa's first nationally representative panel dataset, recent research conclusively reveals that the opportunities available to most South Africans have much to do with the socio-economic status of their family – thus, there is no level-playing field in terms of equality of opportunity in South Africa (Piraino, 2015; Finn et al, 2017). This is manifest in unequal chances of finding work dependent on parental earnings, as well as a high level of persistence between the earnings of fathers and sons. While the average degree of intergenerational persistence in earnings is comparable to other developing countries with similarly high levels of income inequality, what is particular about the South African case is the exceptionally high persistence at the bottom of the earnings distribution. As illustrated in Figure 9.1 below, Finn et al (2017) show that nine out of ten children from the poorest families still occupy the same place in the earnings distribution as their parents did once they themselves enter the labour market. This means that disadvantage is being inherited between generations in South Africa. On the other hand, looking at the top of the distribution, advantage is being passed on too. Children of top-earning fathers have a 70% chance of being at the very top of the earnings distribution themselves. Interestingly, positions in the middle of the earnings distribution appear to be the least stable; testifying to elevated chances of both upward and downward mobility and a relatively high extent of variability among those in the literal middle of the earnings distribution in South Africa.

Figure 9.1: The intergenerational transmission of earnings advantages or disadvantages

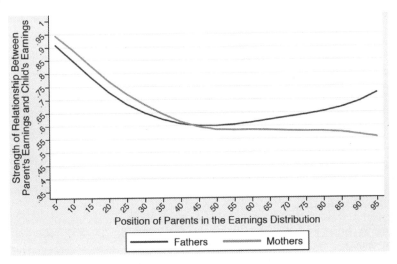

An important question to ask is why there is such little mobility at the bottom of the earnings distribution, even though, since 1994, there has been a rapid increase in average levels of educational attainment in South Africa. Finn et al (2017) offer two interrelated explanations. First, the returns to education increase with educational level and this has worsened over the post-apartheid years. This implies that additional education has a much stronger proportionate impact on earnings at higher levels than at lower levels of education – and the highest returns are being realised by the small share of South Africans with post-secondary education. Second, there is a mismatch between the skills demanded by employers and the content and quality of education that children receive at primary and secondary levels. Thus, while greater access to tertiary education presents a desirable long-term objective, it has to start with significant improvements in the quality of primary and secondary schooling. Closing the gap in educational attainment, while at the same time providing more and better employment opportunities for less skilled workers, will be essential tools to tackle the intergenerational persistence of poverty and inequality in the country.

The intergenerational persistence in earnings – particularly at the lower and the upper extreme of the distribution – should, however, not obscure the substantial extent of volatility that some South Africans experience throughout their lives. In this regard, it is important to highlight that poverty affects many more people in South Africa than a snapshot of poverty at one point in time would suggest.[21] In the four waves of NIDS panel data collected between 2008 and 2014/15, the average poverty rate was around 62%. However, as Figure 9.2 illustrates, 78% of the South African population found themselves in a situation of poverty at least once during the seven years covered

---

21 The remainder of this chapter closely draws on the authors' contribution to the World Bank's South Africa Poverty and Inequality Assessment report (Sulla & Zikhali, 2018). The statistics and conclusions presented here also informed a policy brief prepared for the Institut Français des Relations Internationals (Schotte et al, 2017b).

by these four waves. 39% of all South Africans, 21.7 million people, were persistently poor. Another 39% moved in and out of poverty over time. This precarious mobility is manifest in high probabilities of moving across the poverty line temporarily, but low probabilities of moving away from poverty permanently – that is, an enduringly high degree of vulnerability to slipping into poverty over time.

Figure 9.2: Poverty dynamics in South Africa, 2008–2014/15

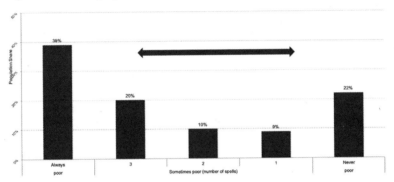

Source: Sulla & Zikhali, 2018
Note: Households are classified as poor if their monthly household consumption per person falls below Statistics South Africa's upper bound poverty line set at R963 (in January 2015 prices).

The reasons why policymakers should care about this precarious mobility are manifold: First, to fight poverty in the long run, poverty escapes must be sustained over time. Second, evidence from the psychological and health literature has revealed that the economic insecurity associated with being vulnerable to poverty reduces people's well-being, even if a deterioration in material welfare does not materialise (see, for example, Cafiero & Vakis, 2006). In other words, it is not only current earnings or consumption that matter for actual welfare, 'but also the risks a household faces, as well as its (in)ability to prevent, mitigate and cope with these' (Klasen & Povel,

2013: 17). Third, vulnerability has the potential to create poverty traps. To be more specific, a high ex-ante risk to poverty can lead people to opt for stable, low-return sources of income, rather than to invest in activities with more lucrative but also more uncertain outcomes (Dercon, 2006; Cafiero & Vakis, 2006).

Given these dynamic considerations, we propose a social stratification schema that aims to capture the existence of structured inequalities in both present living standards and mobility patterns (see Schotte et al, 2017a). The above discussion has highlighted the need to take the distribution of opportunities to move up and risks to slide down the social ladder explicitly into consideration when analysing the persistence of social structures in South Africa. Accordingly, the proposed framework differentiates five social classes:[22] the chronic poor, characterised by high poverty persistence; the transient poor, who have above-average chances of escaping poverty; the non-poor but vulnerable, whose basic needs are currently being met but who face above-average risks of slipping into poverty; the middle class, who are in a better position to maintain a non-poor standard of living even in the event of negative shocks; and the elite, whose living standards situate them far above the average.

Applying this conceptual framework to the South African case using NIDS panel data, we find that only one out of four South Africans can be considered stably middle class or elite, whereas the other three are either poor or vulnerable to falling into poverty. At 20%, South Africa's stable middle class is considerably smaller and its growth has been more sluggish than most existing studies suggest – especially those that locate the middle class just above the poverty line (see Zizzamia et al, 2016). At the same time, we find that the

---

22   As common practice in the development economics literature, in this chapter, we use the term 'class' to describe economic strata. Specifically, these strata delineate economic groups that fall within (i) a defined range of household expenditure per capita and (ii) a defined range of expected poverty risks.

transient poor and the vulnerable, at 27%, constitute a substantial share of the South African population. These two groups straddle the poverty line – with their members frequently moving in and out of poverty – and are similar in their observed characteristics. In this regard, the perspective that our social-stratification schema affords us is valuable in that it challenges the meaningfulness, in a dynamic sense, of the standard division of society into poor and non-poor groups. The transient poor and vulnerable groups nevertheless remain outnumbered by the chronic poor, who – given the past decade's slow economic growth – still constitute the lion's share of the South African population at close to 50%.

As highlighted in the preceding chapters of this book, apartheid imposed a rigid racialised system of unequal resource distribution on the South African society, and the consequences of decades of discriminatory policies persist in enduring spatial and racial dimensions of poverty and deprivation. These patterns are also reflected in the composition of South Africa's five social classes. In this sense, race remains a strong predictor of poverty and the chronically poor group is almost exclusively made up of black and coloured South Africans. These two groups also constitute most of the transient poor and the vulnerable. Although black South Africans also account for the largest proportion of the middle class – with a growing trend in recent years as illustrated in Figure 3 – their share among the two top groups remains far from demographic representative. That is, while black South Africans make up about 80% of the total population, in 2014/15 they made up just above 50% of the middle class. On the other hand, while whites constitute a mere 10% of the South African population, almost one in three members of the middle class and two in three members of the elite are white.

Figure 9.3: Racial composition of South Africa's five social classes, 2008 and 2014/15

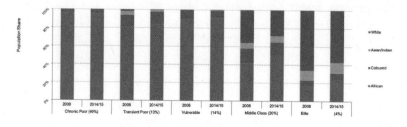

Source: Schotte et al, 2017a

Furthermore, reflecting the spatial legacies of apartheid, chronic poverty remains concentrated in remote and deep rural areas – particularly in the former Bantustans – in provinces such as Limpopo, the Eastern Cape and KwaZulu-Natal. However, although pockets of deep poverty persist in rural regions, it is important to note that the geography of poverty is increasingly shifting as a result of de-agrarianisation, rural to urban migration and high population growth in cities (see Ivan Turok in this volume). In this regard, while rural to urban migration remains effective as a means of improving economic opportunity and living standards, the effectiveness of this mechanism may have decreased as the absorptive capacity of South African cities has failed to keep up with urban population growth. In consequence, rapid urbanisation has left many on the fringes of society. This is manifest in the predominantly urban location of the transient poor and the vulnerable group.

In terms of demographic characteristics, we find that members of households that are female headed, less educated and have a larger number of dependents face a higher risk of poverty, and are thus less likely to enter the ranks of the middle class. Furthermore, as Figure 9.4 displays, access to stable labour market income is a key determinant for achieving economic stability in South Africa. On the downside, members of households where the household head is unemployed or economically inactive, are likely to be either poor or vulnerable. In addition, higher job insecurity can present an important source of vulnerability. Most household heads in the middle class and elite are formally employed with a permanent work contract and union coverage. Among the vulnerable and the transient poor class, by contrast, time-limited work contracts and casual employment are more common. These less stable employment relationships are associated with an elevated risk to poverty.

Figure 9.4: Economic activity of the household head by social class, 2008–2014/15

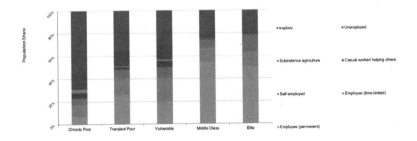

Source: Schotte et al, 2017a.

Based on the detected class characteristics (see Schotte et al, 2017a for a more detailed discussion), the proposed stratification schema can provide important information for policy-makers with respect to the design and targeting of social policies. Our analysis shows that the chronic poor are characterised by exceptionally low levels of human capital and financial assets as well as their geographical isolation from markets and employment opportunities. These characteristics make them unlikely candidates for fruitful integration into the prevailing economy in the short term. However, ensuring a basic degree of economic security and service provision for this group will be a necessary precondition for ensuring that their health, education and nutritional needs are met. In addition to the provision of basic services, cash transfers will remain an indispensable source of income for many of South Africa's chronic poor.

The detected high level of churning around the poverty line presents another complex policy challenge. Those economically insecure households that straddle the poverty line are especially in need of effective mechanisms to cope with economic vulnerability, and, compared to the chronic poor, are also more likely candidates for integration into the productive economy with the appropriate social policy interventions. This group is more urban, better educated and relies more heavily on income earned in the labour market than those experiencing poverty as a persistent state. Like the chronic poor, this group stands to benefit from a base level of stability provided by state social policy. However, this is not enough to keep them stably out of poverty. We show that the economic instability this group experiences is closely linked to their vulnerable position in the labour market. Historically and in eras of near full employment, an unemployment insurance fund has been a key mechanism to mediate such vulnerability to tide workers over between jobs. Moreover, it is the transient poor and the vulnerable that would benefit most from employment growth and a policy focus on improving employment security for workers in currently precarious forms of employment. In this regard, policymakers are likely to face an important trade-off between labour market arrangements to foster quick job creation, and a longer-run project of creating better and more stable jobs that will allow more South Africans to escape poverty over the longer term.

References

Cafiero, C. & R. Vakis. 2006. 'Risk and vulnerability considerations in poverty analysis: Recent advances and future directions', Social Protection Discussion Paper 0610, The World Bank, Washington.

Dercon, S. 2006. 'Vulnerability: A micro perspective', in F. Bourguignon, B. Pleskovic & J. van der Gaag, eds. *Securing Development in an Unstable World*. Washington: World Bank Publications, pp. 117–46.

Finn, A., M. Leibbrandt & V. Ranchhod. 2017. 'atterns of persistence: Intergenerational mobility and education in South Africa', SALDRU Working Paper Number 175/ NIDS Discussion Paper 2016/2. Version 2, SALDRU, Cape Town.

Klasen, S. & F. Povel. 2013. Defining and measuring vulnerability: State of the art and new proposals', in S. Klasen & H. Povel, Eds. *Vulnerability to Poverty*. London: Palgrave, pp. 17–49.

Piraino, P. 2015. 'Intergenerational earnings mobility and equality of opportunity in South Africa'. *World Development*, 67: 396–405.

Schotte, S., R. Zizzamia & M. Leibbrandt. 2017a. 'Social stratification, life chances and vulnerability to poverty in South Africa', SALDRU Working Paper Number 208, SALDRU, Cape Town.

Schotte, S., R. Zizzamia & M. Leibbrandt. 2017b. 'Defining the middle class in the global south: A quantitative perspective from South Africa', *Ifri, L'Afrique en questions*, 33: 1–6.

Sulla, V. & P. Zikhali. 2018. *Overcoming Poverty and Inequality in South Africa: An Assessment of Drivers, Constraints and Opportunities*. Washington, D.C.: World Bank Group.

Zizzamia, R., S. Schotte, M. Leibbrandt & V. Ranchhod. 2016. 'Vulnerability and the middle class in South Africa', SALDRU Working Paper Number 188/ NIDS Discussion Paper 2016/15, SALDRU, Cape Town.

CONCLUSION

Michael Nassen Smith

THE ESSAYS COLLECTED IN THIS VOLUME have stressed the necessity and urgency of confronting inequality in South Africa. Each essay has proposed a number of concrete policy solutions towards that end; some narrowly focused and sector specific, others more broad and cross-cutting. The space to evaluate each of these, and the intellectual work that went into producing them, is beyond the scope of this conclusion. This is a task that must be taken up by academics, researchers, policymakers and activists in the years to come. Nonetheless, it might be useful to list a few salient theses:

- Inequality is deeply embedded in South Africa's social structure and is a largely a consequence of the country's colonial and apartheid history and present-day policy failures.
- Advantage and disadvantage is largely inherited and significant state support is needed to assist the chronic poor to escape poverty.
- South Africa has failed to take advantage of a post-apartheid era demographic dividend.
- South Africans live 'in different worlds' and it is imperative to address the geography of inequality in the country.
- Wage inequality is excessive and unsustainable, with South African

162

CEO salaries in relation to ordinary workers far exceeding what is morally, politically and economically just.

- South Africa will remain prone to political manipulation by nefarious interests if inequality is not resolved.

With these points in mind, we believe that it is crucial to emphasise the need for a structural transformation of South Africa's economy. Inequality is a function of the systematic failure of post-apartheid macroeconomic and industrial policy to realise the aspirations of the country's majority and resolve the social divisions persisting from the apartheid era. As Bell et al (2018) argue, industrial policy and reindustrialisation should be placed at the centre of South Africa's development strategy. This strategy must overcome the interests of a narrow coalition of elites that have determined the trajectory of the economy since the transition. Such policy will need to encompass significant public investment and direction, and must entail the final abandonment of 'trickle-down' economics, a paradigm that has unfortunately dominated policy thinking in the democratic era (Padayachee, 2018). One should hasten to add that any industrial policy must be sensitive to the demands of the current ecological crisis and the reality of climate change.

Whether or not the South African state is able to embark on the ambitious reforms needed to confront poverty, unemployment and inequality is another question. The state's ability to do so will naturally require a renewal of our democratic institutions and the capabilities of our administrative organs. This necessitates a comprehensive attack on 'state capture' in all of its manifestations, a project that is encouraged in this volume, particularly by Thuli Madonsela and Kgalema Motlanthe.

Inequality is not merely a technical problem and resolving it will require going beyond the identification and application of appropriate technical solutions. Rather, confronting inequality must involve the mobilisation of progressive forces across government, civil society, academia, trade unions and social movements. One of the strongest criticisms of Piketty's *Capital in the 21st Century* was that it did not illuminate, despite Piketty's best intentions, the political and ideological forces behind the reproduction of inequality (Boushey et al, 2017). Piketty's framework was therefore rather limited. As a result, he did not fully explore the social dimensions of the necessary fight against inequality.

In a commentary on responses to *Capital in the 21st Century*, Piketty acknowledged this weakness and has since called for a reconciliation between economics and the social sciences. Moreover, he has maintained that the analysis undertaken in his celebrated work should be seen as a starting point; an incomplete and unfinished project (Piketty, 2017). The large interest and response shown to *Capital in the 21st Century* from across history, political science, sociology and other disciplines hopefully signals the beginnings of an ambitious academic project that extends into the global South, where Piketty's work, as mentioned in the Preface to this volume, does not venture of its own accord.

There are a number of projects underway in South Africa in line with the imperative to broaden the scope of inequality studies specifically and the teaching of economics more broadly. The Rethinking Economics for Africa (REFA) movement, a local chapter of an international project, was launched in 2018 under the guidance of the newly formed Institute for Economic Justice (IEJ) and has the support of students, academics and several institutes in civil society, including the Institute for African Alternatives (IFAA). REFA is promoting pluralism, political economy and interdisciplinary thinking within economics and this will, in our view, enhance researchers' ability to understand inequality in all of its dimensions. In addition, the recently formed Southern Centre for Inequality Studies adds to the intellectual arsenal needed to confront the phenomenon of inequality systematically and from the perspective of the global South.

There are specific research gaps worth mentioning before we close. First is wealth: Who has it, how is it maintained and how it is reproduced? These questions, we believe, present a fertile research agenda. On a political and social register, the potential for the wealthy in driving political directions and economic structures is an acute concern in the South African context in which inequality is already so extreme. In response, Terreblanche (2018) has already motivated for a wealth tax. Second, the South African economy is going through a period of intense financialisation, as alluded to in Makgetla's contribution to this volume. While there is a growing literature on this phenomenon (Ashman et al, 2013; Newman, 2014; Isaacs, 2016), there is room to link it directly with the question of inequality in South Africa.

Work on inequality in South Africa must naturally include a focus on gender, racial and class issues. Thinking through the cross-cutting dimensions of inequality and its relationship to the political, ideological and social might be framed as an 'intersectional' imperative, to borrow from a term that is in vogue today. A specific word, however, might be valuable on the question of race and racial inequality. Given ubiquitous racial inequities and racialised consciousness inherited from South Africa's past, researchers should be given the vocabulary to engage not only in the racialised economic outcomes, but also in sociological and philosophical questions regarding the construction of race and identity in social discourse and the consequence (or unintended consequences) of well-meaning policy formulations (Alexander, 2013; Mare, 2014; Erasmus, 2017).

In South African political economic historiography, scholarship undertaken during the apartheid era, by Harold Wolpe, Martin Legassick and others, was in keeping with the imperative to think at the intersection of the political, economic, social and ideological

(Bond, 2010). Yet that tradition has fallen away, certainly within the discipline of economics. A revival of political economy would certainly be welcome. This revival will need to concern itself with the international dimensions of inequality and the intersection between national economic conditions and South Africa's current integration into the global capitalist economic and political system. There is great scope for conversation between economists, political scientists and international relations specialists on this front.

As already mentioned, we need to understand what social forces and alliances are necessary to force through the ambitious structural reforms needed to address inequality in South Africa. Piketty claimed that the equalising period in the West during, what he calls, the 'Golden Social Democratic Age,' was due to declining power of the former plutocratic elite in that region. In contemporary South Africa, how might power be redistributed away from the incumbent elite and towards the interests of the country's working poor and socially marginalised? This is a question for social movements, government and civil society as much as it is for engaged intellectuals and academics. Confronting inequality, in sum, is a research, academic, moral and political imperative. We hope this volume aids the struggle against inequality specifically and economic justice more broadly, across all of these dimensions.

References

Alexander, N. 2013. *Thoughts on New South Africa*. Johannesburg: Jacana Media.

Ashman, S., S. Mohamed & S. Newman. 2013. 'The *financialisation of the South African economy and its impact on economic growth and employment*', Discussion Paper, UNDESA, Geneva. Available at: http://eprints.uwe.ac.uk/32370 [Accessed on 17 October 2018].

Bell, J., S. Goga, P. Mondliwa & S. Roberts.2018. 'Structural transformation in South Africa: Moving towards a smart, open economy for all',

Industrial Development Think Tank (IDTT). Available at: https:// static1.squarespace.com/static/52246331e4b0a46e5f1b8ce5/t/5 ad9e4baf950b767531fe8a9/1524229357942/IDTT+Structural+ Transformation+in+South+Africa+Moving+towards+a+smart%2C+ open+economy+for+all.pdf [Accessed on 1 August 2018].

Bond, P. 2010. 'A half century of competing political economic traditions in South Africa', Paper presented at 'Race, Class and the Developmental State', 16 November, 2010, Port Elizabeth. Available at: http://ccs.ukzn. ac.za/files/Bond%20Legassick%20poli%20econ%20conference%20 paper.pdf [Accessed on 1 September 2018].

Boushey, H., B. de Long & M. Steinhum, ed. 2017. *After Piketty: The Agenda for Economics and Inequality.* Cambridge: Harvard University Press.

Erasmus, Z. 2017. *Race Otherwise: Forging a New Humanism for South Africa.* Johannesburg: Wits University Press.

Isaacs, G. 2016. 'Financialisation and development: South African case study'. FESSUD Working Paper May 2016.

Mare, G. 2014. *Declassified: Moving Beyond the Dead End of Race in South Africa.* Johannesburg: Jacana Media.

Newman, S. 2014. 'Financialisation and the financial and economic crisis: The case of South Africa', FESSUD Project Report.

Padayachee, V. 2018. 'Beyond a treasury view of the world: Reflections from theory and history on heterodox policy options for South Africa', SCIS Working Paper, 2. Available at: https://www.wits.ac.za/media/ wits-university/faculties-and-schools/commerce-law-and-management/ research-entities/scis/documents/SCISWorkingpaper2.pdf [Accessed on 2 September 2018]

Piketty, T. 2017. 'Towards a reconciliation between economics and the social sciences', in H. Boushey, B. de Long & M. Steinhum, ed. 2017. *After Piketty: The Agenda for Economics and Inequality.* Cambridge: Harvard University Press.

AUTHOR BIOGRAPHIES

David Francis

David Francis is the research manager at the Southern Centre for Inequality Studies at the University of the Witwatersrand and is a researcher in economics in the faculty of commerce, law and management at Wits. He is a research associate on the CSID National Minimum Wage-Research Initiative with a focus on wage inequality. He has a Master's degree in development studies from the University of KwaZulu-Natal and an undergraduate degree in history and economics from University of Cape Town. In 2016 he was appointed as the researcher for the National Minimum Wage Advisory Panel. He is currently reading for a doctorate in labour market economics, which examines the South African labour market from a structural perspective.

Pali Lehohla

Dr Pali Lehohla was the statistician general of South Africa, a position he held from 2000 to 2017. He was the chair of Africa Symposium for Statistical Development (ASSD), a country-led initiative established in 2006. He was the chair of the United Nations Statistics Commission, the Statistics Commission and the PARIS21. He obtained his first degree from the National University of Lesotho with double majors in statistics and economics, undertook postgraduate studies in demography from the United Nations Regional Institute for Population Studies (UNRIPS) at the University of Ghana and the senior executive programme jointly awarded by Wits and Harvard universities. Dr Lehohla holds honorary doctorates from the University of Stellenbosch and the University of KwaZulu-Natal.

Murray Leibbrandt

Murray Leibbrandt is the pro vice-chancellor of the University of Cape Town. He holds the Department of Science and Technology/National Research Foundation Research Chair in Poverty and Inequality Research. He is the director of the Southern Africa Labour and Development Research Unit at the University of Cape Town's school of economics. He serves on the executive committee of the International Economic Association and is a senior research fellow of the World Institute for Development Economics (WIDER) and the Institute for Labor Economics (IZA). He is a member of the Academy of Science of South Africa (ASSAf) and from 2014 to 2017 chaired the ASSAf Standing Committee on Science for the Alleviation of Poverty and Inequality. In 1995 and 1996 he served on President Mandela's Labour Market Commission to advise on post-apartheid labour market legislation and then, in 2016 and 2017, served on the deputy president's advisory panel on the national minimum wage.

His research gathers and uses longitudinal survey data to track South Africans over time in order to analyse the poverty, inequality and labour market dynamics of contemporary South Africa. He is one of the principal investigators of the Department of Planning, Monitoring and Evaluation's National Income Dynamics Study. As UCT's pro vice-chancellor, Leibbrandt headed the management team for the Mandela Initiative on Strategies to Overcome Poverty and Inequality.

Thuli Madonsela

Thulisile 'Thuli' Madonsela is the Law Trust chair in social justice and a law professor at the University of Stellenbosch. She is also the founder of the Thuma Foundation, an independent democracy leadership and literacy social enterprise. An advocate of the High Court of South Africa, Madonsela has been a lifelong activist on social justice, constitutionalism, human rights, good governance and the rule of law. Named one of TIME's 100 most influential people in the world in 2014 and Forbes Africa Person of the Year 2016, she is one of the drafters of South Africa's Constitution. She recently completed a seven-year term as South Africa's public protector. Before this tenure, Madonsela served in various leadership capacities in civil society and government, including as full-time commissioner in the South African Law Reform Commission. She has five honorary doctor of law degrees. Madonsela is a Paul Harris Fellow, recipient of Transparency International's Integrity Award, the German Africa Prize and Africa Anticorruption Crusader Award, among her innumerable accolades. A Tallberg Global Leader, among others, she spent a year at Harvard in 2017 as an Advanced Leadership Fellow.

Neva Seidman Makgetla

Dr Neva Makgetla has been a senior economist at Trade and Industrial Policy Strategies (TIPS) since November 2015. She was the deputy director general for economic policy in the Economic Development Department (EDD) from 2010 to 2015. Before joining the EDD, Makgetla worked for the Presidency, the Development Bank of Southern Africa and the Congress of the South African Trade Unions as well as other government departments. Prior to 1994 she worked in various universities in Africa and the United States. Makgetla's research centres on aspects of industrial policy and value chain analysis, and on socio-economic challenges facing South Africa, especially around employment creation and inequality.

Kaylan Massie

Kaylan Massie is a Canadian barrister and solicitor and graduated with an Honours degree in economics with distinction from Queen's University in 2005. In 2008 she obtained a Bachelor of Laws from the University of British Columbia. After completing her articling qualifications at one of Canada's top corporate and commercial law firms, Davies Ward Phillips and Vineberg LLP, she began practising litigation, labour and employment law at MacPherson Leslie and Tyerman LLP. During her practice, she represented an array of clients before courts, tribunals, labour boards and arbitrators. Following her family's relocation to South Africa, she obtained a Master's degree in South African Labour Law with distinction from the University of Cape Town. She is co-author of the book *Executive Salaries in South Africa: Who should have a say on pay?* published in 2014. Kaylan now lives in London, where she undertakes research and writing projects focused on wages and inequality, most recently writing a wage inequality report published by the National Minimum Wage Research Initiative at the University of the Witwatersrand.

Andrew McGregor

Andrew McGregor is the managing director of Who Owns Whom (WOW). Andrew matriculated from Settlers High School, Cape Town, in 1979 and completed his tertiary education at the Cape Peninsula University of Technology in 1983. On completing his studies, he joined his late father, Robin McGregor, in the recently established publishing business WOW and, apart from a four-year period contracting to the banking industry in the late 1990s, has been there ever since. WOW was traditionally a book publishing business that focused on ownership and is well known for identifying the high concentration of economic ownership in South African business during the apartheid era. The business has re-invented itself a number of times over the last 38 years and now provides a subscription-accessed web-based platform, which researches and publishes the world's largest database of African private companies, industries, directors and management as well as fixed direct investment on the African continent. WOW also researches and produces the Wealth Index for the City Press newspaper and has published a number of papers on corporate transparency, BEE trends, the evolving structure of the private sector and state-owned corporations.

Zunaid Moola

Zunaid Moola is the deputy editor of *New Agenda: South African Journal of Social and Economic Policy*. He previously worked as a consultant specialising in economic development strategies and poverty alleviation. He was the executive director of the New Institute for Economic Policy and the manager of the Service Program in South Africa's first democratic Parliament. He is also a facilitator in the Training for Transformation Programme at the Grail Centre in Kleinmond, Western Cape. Zunaid holds a Master's degree in political economy from the New School of Social Research, New York and a Bachelor's degree in political science from Carleton University, Canada. His interests include alternative economics and economic literacy.

Kgalema Petrus Motlanthe

Kgalema Motlanthe is the former president of the Republic of South Africa who presided over the 2009 general election which marked the end of his term of office. He then served as the deputy president of South Africa for one term from 2009–2014. He has also served as the deputy president of the ANC (2007–2012) and the secretary-general of the ANC (1997–2007).

He was elected as the general secretary of the National Union of Mineworkers NUM in 1992. He also served as the first chairman of the ANC in the Pretoria Witwatersrand Vaal (PWV) Region, which is today Gauteng province. Mkhuluwa (as he is affectionately known) was imprisoned on Robben Island for underground activities of the ANC (1977–1987).

Motlanthe is the patron and chairman of the Kgalema Motlanthe Foundation whose vision is to contribute to the socio-economic development agenda of the peoples of South Africa and the African continent by building and facilitating access to the mainstream domestic and global economy. He also serves as the chairperson of the OR Tambo School of Leadership, which is a leadership school created by the ANC for capacitating its membership, and is chairman of the board of the Institute for African Alternatives (IFAA).

Michael Nassen Smith

Michael Nassen Smith is currently the deputy director of the Institute for African Alternatives (IFAA), having previously lectured at the University of Cape Town in the politics department. He holds an MPhil from the University of Cape Town. His research interests include the history of South African political thought, South African and global political and economic history, political philosophy and the philosophy of race. Michael is eager to connect intellectual work with pursuits for social and economic justice. He is also interested in promoting interdisciplinary work in the academy.

Ben Turok

Professor Ben Turok was a member of Parliament in South Africa representing the ruling African National Congress (ANC). Prof Turok has degrees in engineering, philosophy and political science, and is the author of 20 books on African development economics and politics. Turok was a lecturer at the Open University in London and has taught at many universities across Africa over the years. He has worked closely with the United Nations Economic Commission for Africa and the European Parliamentary Assembly among other bodies. He is currently the director of the Institute for African Alternatives (IFAA) and editor of *New Agenda: South African Journal of Social and Economic Policy.*

Ivan Turok

Ivan Turok is the executive director at the Human Sciences Research Council and is responsible for the Economic Performance and Development programme. He is the editor-in-chief of the international journal, *Regional Studies* and an honorary professor at the University of Glasgow. He is also chairman of the City Planning Commission for Durban. Turok is an urban and regional economist/planner with over 30 years' experience in research, teaching and policy advice. He is an occasional adviser to the United Nations, OECD, African Development Bank, UNECA and several national governments. He was a member of the expert panel that prepared South Africa's Integrated Urban Development Framework. He is the author of over 150 academic publications, journal articles, book chapters and books, many of which are highly cited internationally. His research covers various aspects of city and regional development, labour markets, urbanisation, urban transformation and affordable housing. His latest jointly edited book is called *Transitions in Regional Economic Development* (2018, Routledge).

Rocco Zizzamia

Rocco Zizzamia is a research officer at the Southern African Labour and Development Research Unit (SALDRU). He holds an MPhil in development studies from the University of Oxford. He previously studied economic history at the University of Cape Town. His research interests include the study of poverty and poverty dynamics, labour economics and economic inequality.

Simone Schotte

Simone Schotte is a doctoral research fellow at the GIGA German Institute of Global and Area Studies and a member of the Globalisation and Development (GlaD) research training group at the University of Göttingen. Her main research interests lie in social inequality, social mobility and poverty and class-dynamics. Using South Africa as a case study, in her dissertation she aims to understand the key determinants of economic stability and upward mobility, and explores the main challenges that impede people from escaping poverty sustainably and entering the rank of the middle class. Her work on poverty dynamics and patterns of social stratification in South Africa in collaboration with Prof. Murray Leibbrandt and Rocco Zizzamia was published in *World Development* and featured in a World Bank report, policy briefs, blog posts and news stories.

INDEX